DELIBERATE
PRACTICE

FOR
CREATIVE
WRITERS

JULES HORNE

Texthouse, The Corn Exchange, Woodmarket, Kelso, TD5 7AT

www.texthouse.co.uk

Deliberate Practice for Creative Writers— 1st ed.

Cover art: Cohorts by Design
Cover design: Jules Horne

ISBN
978-1-9149030-3-8 (paperback)
978-1-9149030-4-5 (ebook)

Are you looking for a fast, effective way to improve your writing? Transform your technique with bitesize deliberate practice.

For writing tips and inspiration, join the mailing list at www.method-writing.com

IDENTIFY THE ISSUE.
CREATE A SHORT FEEDBACK LOOP.
PRACTISE.

Contents

Introduction

Are you looking for a quick, effective way to improve your writing?

A way that's fast. Focused. Impactful.

A methodology that's

* systematic
* backed by research
* used by educators to sky-rocket student writing skills
* adaptable to your style and genre
* great for studying how writers achieve their effects.

That way is deliberate practice.

Deliberate practice is the art of identifying a problem area, homing in, and giving it dedicated attention. Think of it as sports reps or music practice for writers.

A little deliberate practice can transform your writing toolkit.

And it's backed by academic research into the science of excellence.

I've used it to learn writing tactics from William Shakespeare, Angela Carter, Stephen King, and many others. I've used it for close reading and technique study which have helped me to write and edit with confidence. I've introduced deliberate practice successfully to writing students, and now I'm sharing my discoveries in this book.

I hope it'll help you to improve your craft, learn new writing tools, and make discoveries of your own that you can put into practice right away.

Get ready to raise your game!

Deliberate Practice – Your Secret Superpower

Deliberate practice means systematic learning, broken into small chunks of study.

Maybe you've heard of *10,000 hours* – the idea that it takes 10,000 hours to become an expert in a new field? Or you've read Malcolm Gladwell's book *Outliers*? They're essentially about the power of deliberate practice. And the good news is, you don't need 10,000 hours. Far from it!

Have you ever trained in a sport, or dance, or playing a musical instrument? Then you've already done deliberate practice.

Have you heard of the chess prodigies, the Polgar sisters? Deliberate practice turned them into world champions.

Deliberate practice is also used in the art world. Students copy old masters to study their techniques. When artist Paul Klee[1] taught artists how to draw, he captured his ideas in inspiring sketchbooks which are still studied today – and they use a deliberate practice approach.

Deliberate practice goes by different names in different activities. In sport and fitness – *reps* and *stretches*. In music – *scales* and *études*. In art – *sketches* and *studies*. In meditation – *practice*.

It's not a new concept. But it's rarely applied to writing.

I'll look at why later on.

But meanwhile, ask yourself: what if you could apply these proven techniques to your writing?

Well, you can. More and more schools and colleges are now teaching this approach, based on sound research.

So, that's what this book is about – the theory and practice of deliberate practice for writing. I've chosen a particular focus on creative writing here, but the techniques can equally be used for other genres.

In this book, you'll learn

* how to use deliberate practice to develop your own writing style
* how to solve your writing issues, and progress faster
* how to learn techniques from Stephen King, Maya Angelou, Shakespeare… any writer or genre you choose!

I once spent a summer harvesting writing advice from Shakespeare. Hilary Mantel, John Irving and Ray Bradbury have also helped. Learning techniques from these amazing writers has really helped my own writing.

And you can put your learning to work right away in your work in progress. Simply:

* analyse the technique
* break it into tiny elements, and
* practise.

Just as a violinist, footballer or chess player learns a new move, and then practises till it's second nature.

Of course, every writer is different, just as every gymnast or pianist is different. You're unique, so you'll want to focus on your individual needs.

This book provides a flexible approach you can adapt to your own interests, genre and style.

I'll also give examples from my own deliberate practice, which you can use, borrow or adapt to suit you.

And the great news? You don't need to spend 10,000 hours. Just a few minutes a day will make a difference. Just as a few daily minutes of exercise, music or sports training will shift the dial on your skill level. If you've ever read *Tiny Habits*[2] – Prof B.J. Fogg's ground-breaking strategy for making powerful changes –

you'll know what I'm talking about. More on this and other major research later.

I appreciate that everyone has their own learning style, and you may not want to start at the beginning. You may prefer to try something hands-on, and read the theory later. That's fine, though do return to the theory – I found it incredibly helpful for understanding patterns of resistance and what's going on the brain.

Here's a map so you can quickly find what interests you most.

If you'd like to start creating your own deliberate practice patterns, feel free to jump ahead to **Part 3: Doing Deliberate Practice**.

Or, cut straight to the chase and try some patterns I've already gathered from my own active reading, including writing techniques from famous writers. These are in **Part 4: Deliberate Practice Examples**. They'll help to you get ideas for your own writing discovery.

In **Part 5: Language Topics**, you'll find deliberate practice examples gathered under different language and craft themes, including *parts of speech, time* and *space*. These cover frequent craft issues, and will give you a starting-point to help with areas you might want to tackle in your own writing.

Part 6: Shape & Pattern gathers playful concepts and techniques, including *blackouts*, *net bags*, *signal-to-noise ratio*, and the maverick French experimenters *Oulipo*. Think of it as a kind of lab for writing adventurers. This is a great place to go for a refresh, or creative experiments.

Part 6 also has a section on artificial intelligence (AI). This is, of course, evolving at superspeed. I've experimented with where AI can be useful as a co-creator, supporting your human, hand-crafted, brain-crafted writing. I've found that it really excels as a teacher and learning partner. It has astounding patience, and encyclopaedic bookish knowledge. Though when I asked what day it is today, it got it wrong! And on the writing front, it's still very much a learner. Head to **Part 6** for my findings so far.

Part 7: Writing Visualisation opens a new frontier, with a look at visual tools that show what's going on below the surface of words, designed to help you to plan, write and edit more effectively. This section includes tools such as colour-coding, helicopter vision, wallpaper rolls, and my own innovative text visualisation app, **Textvizz**. Find out more at **www.textvizz.com**.

And finally, if you're a teacher, or a student of growth and productivity, head for **Part 8: The Science of Excellence.** It brings together an overview of some leading experts in the field, including Anders Ericsson, B.J. Fogg, Carol Dweck and Malcolm Gladwell, with some thoughts on how their research can be applied to writing.

But before that, in **Part 2: About Deliberate Practice,** you'll find an overview of the cornerstones: what deliberate practice is, how it works, and why it works. Even if you jump ahead to try some examples, you'll want to return here later, to learn the process and key concepts.

And because this book is about deliberate practice *for writing*, to set the context, in the **Introduction**, I go into my experiences as a trainee writer in journalism, editorial and scriptwriting – which was a big leap for a wee bookish kid with no background in the writing industries. Then, I share something of what I've learned from many years of teaching writing at a UK university.

And it's important to add that while this book was written for adult learners, the techniques apply just as well to younger learners, and are being used with great success in modern teaching and learning in schools and colleges.

Deliberate practice and superlearning – learning how to learn – are changing the game throughout education, and that includes writing.[3]

In writing this book, I've sometimes drawn on educational thinking from music, and from the artist Paul Klee, of the *Bauhaus* art and design school. Recent developments in language visualisation have also inspired new thinking.

I hope that by exploring language and writing in more depth, you'll be excited by your discoveries, and gain more confidence in your craft.

Why do deliberate practice?

I often hear the writing advice: "write the book you want to read". Well, that's this book. It's one I sorely needed when I was starting out, but it didn't exist.

It's about a level of writing craft learning that in my view comes too late.

Early on, like most aspiring writers, I went to writers' groups. I heard a lot of people read their work, but rarely picked up solid craft tips.

Then I got published. I never got solid editorial advice.

Looking back at that early writing, I cringe at its bagginess. Its self-indulgence. That's fine! It's beginner work. But no one ever took me aside and pointed and said: *rookie error.*

And I wanted to hear it!

I didn't get that professional editorial feedback until I worked in the writing industries. Journalism, scriptwriting, copywriting. The writing issues are surprisingly similar. And so are the solutions. So the thinking behind this book is: what solutions might be more helpful for adult learners than the current "learning by osmosis" approach?

At this point, a disclaimer. Nobody's perfect, and certainly not me. There's clearly no such thing as a perfect writer, or perfect writing. I love Leonard Cohen's wisdom:

> *"There's a crack in everything. That's where the light gets in."*

We're all works in progress, and you decide your own process and idea of success.

The beauty of deliberate practice is that it's a learning *system*. You can diagnose what you need, tune to what you're interested in, and create your own bitesize, highly focused learning.

I've been sharing some of my own discoveries with writers on my mailing list, and they've found it very helpful:

> *"I used your tips to give the reader a snapshot of the new characters from the protagonist's POV... This was a*

great tip that prevented me from going into long physical descriptions in a scene in the novel that needs to retain conflict, tension and creeping dread."
Paula G, MA student

If you're interested in subscribing, go to **www.method-writing.com**. You can also email me at **info@method-writing.com**.

I'd love to hear what you discover using your new superpower: deliberate practice.

About Me

I'm a fiction, stage and radio writer, and for over a decade, I taught creative writing at The Open University, the world's largest distance learning university, and was also on the course writing team for the MA in Creative Writing. Before that, I worked in BBC journalism and translation.

So, I've trained and worked professionally in different forms and genres of writing – what's known as *multimodal* writing. I'm from Scotland, and have a geeky interest in music, creative technology, and learning how things work behind the scenes, which has probably influenced this book!

You'll find more information on my website, **www.method-writing.com**.

A quick word about where I'm coming from. No writer arrives ready-formed, and most have a background of struggles and self-doubt to work their way through.

Like many writers, I was a book-devourer at a very young age. We had only a handful of books at home, and I was so thirsty to read. I relied heavily on the local children's librarian, the wonderful Alma. I still remember discovering Frank L. Baum and realising there were *other Wizard of Oz books*.

I never thought I could be a writer. But I had a great primary teacher, Mr John Stables, a big, bearded bloke from Manchester, who gave me my first steps in creative writing. He opened a whole world of imagination and possibility. And I stuck at it.

Fast-forward through the lean college years, where I was far too intimidated by studying literature to actually write myself.

And fast-forward again, via journalism, and a lovely supportive local writer in residence, and I'm still writing, and earning my living from it. I've won fiction and playwriting awards, and had plays and stories on BBC Radio. It hasn't always been easy, but I've kept going.

But I want to tell you about something I did one summer. It was hot, and I was sitting in a small office room, stealing a famous writer's secrets.

A summer of stealing Shakespeare

Although I wrote plays, I always had imposter syndrome, because I didn't know anything about Shakespeare. Like many kids, I'd toughed my way through reading some of his plays at school, but didn't understand much, or get much joy from it.

Whenever I met someone with a theatre background, I felt embarrassed. Eventually I thought: "I've got to do something about this."

So, I did a Shakespeare course online, with The Open University. The same Shakespeare course as the British comedian Lenny Henry: *Shakespeare: Text and Performance.* He did it for similar reasons: to fill in a gap.

So, to cut a long story short. I spent a summer dissecting Shakespeare plays. Not as a student – as a writer.

I had this huge book of his plays, and scribbled in it furiously, underlining, making notes. Marking bits I loved with exclamation marks. Not the famous bits or the poetic bits. The writing techniques. *Viewpoint, imagery, dialogue, scene cuts.*

I watched plays and films of plays, too. From black-and-white classic movies to online National Theatre. Again, viewing as a writer. *Structure, scene, metaphor, rhythm.*

Every now and then, I spotted something, and said: "Aha! That's what you're up to. Very cunning, Will." I took notes.

So, for example, Shakespeare has this great trick for introducing a character and creating tension. He doesn't just have Macbeth stride in, and everyone falls at his feet. Oh no.

This is how Shakespeare introduces Macbeth, the man who would be king:

The other soldiers are talking about this guy off-stage – a hardcore psycho killer. A guy who carved a soldier open from chin to belly with his sword, in one swift motion. What's this hardcore psycho killer guy's name? Macbeth.

Wow! You've got my attention. When Macbeth eventually comes on stage, everyone's blood runs cold.

Shakespeare uses a similar technique with Cleopatra. She's quite the opposite. She's the powerful, seductive queen of Egypt. Shakespeare introduces her, once again, not in person, but reported indirectly by other characters.

Long before she appears, the crowd scent her heady, exotic perfume on the wind. The sails of her golden barge are thick with perfume. And we hear how she sailed past, in her gold pavilion, surrounded by her nymph-like maids, and cupid-boys with fans.

What an entrance! She isn't anywhere near the stage yet. And it's done entirely through other people speaking about her. Cleopatra doesn't need to lift a finger.

The audience are dying to see these characters, and neither Cleopatra nor Macbeth have said a word.

So, that's an example of a writing technique I noted from Shakespeare. But this kind of gold-mining works for any writer, in any genre.

Plundering Stephen King

Reading Stephen King as a writer, I found he has a trick of spinning words together to create new ones:

That was stupid. Nothing but shock-think.

The old lady with the beauty-shop curls.

The throat-biting teenage girl.

16

He pointed to a green-painted kiosk.[4]

The effect is compact, and lands the stress on the noun at the end of the sentence, giving it more salience. This language structure reminds me of German, which easily combines word elements into complex adjectives.

King has another distinctive technique using visual shorthand to set up anonymous characters:

> *The little guy with the mustache… the little man with the mustache… the short man with the mustache… the little man…*
>
> *The man in the tattered shirt… the man in the shredded shirt…*

He also turns visual qualities into nicknames:

> *Power Suit Woman… Mister Softee Guy…*[5]

This technique allows him to paint pictures, helping to keep a visual sense of a secondary character alive in the reader's imagination. This in turn helps with flow and signposting.

It's a good example of a technique you might want to play with and adapt to your own way of writing.

Harvesting John le Carré

John le Carré, the British spy thriller novelist, has an interesting way of flowing time and place. It's not just the story and characters that sweep you along. It's also a specific use of language which pulls you forward with momentum, even in scenes where there isn't much action.

He does this by creating long spans of words that link together, rather like the rise and fall of musical phrasing. So, when you've read the first part of the sentence which ends with a comma and an unresolved feeling (deep breath), you're impelled to read on to get the second part.

A bit like I've just done there, but with more sophistication!

Le Carré has a few distinctive temporal patterns like this. For example, here's the use of the past perfect (*had*) to sketch in backstory:

> *It was April. Smiley had come back from Portugal, where he had been burying a scandal, to find…*
>
> *From the outset of this meeting Smiley had assumed for the main a Buddha-like inscrutability…*[6]

Again, he creates a feeling of something unresolved which needs completion.

Le Carré also uses *past continuous* verbs, also called the *past progressive* – for example, *she was running, they were shouting*.

As the name suggests, *past continuous* combines past and still ongoing action. The effect is to evoke the past, and pull it through into the present. This puts us in the middle of things[7], which helps us to feel time on the move, and a sense of being immersed in an active scene.

> *Jim was addressing them all, making light of it now.*
>
> *Mendel was still holding onto the briefcase.*

It's a simple language structure with a powerful impact.

Another le Carré technique is the use of *verbal adjectives* – for example, *growing concern, mounting interest*. Here, the action verb is turned into an adjective, implying escalation or change:

> *With mounting interest… he had a growing feeling…*[8]

Powerful techniques like this are hidden in every writer's work. They're under the radar unless you look closely, as a writer. But even as a casual reader, you certainly feel that undercurrent.

To cut a long story short, by close-reading favourite writers and analysing some of their techniques, I gained some very useful skills – skills I was able to use right away.

Deliberate practice hacking like this is straightforward, and fits well into small pockets of time. You can even multitask and gather examples while doing other things – waiting for a train, watching TV, listening to the radio.

So, let's get started!

Capturing Writing Craft Techniques

Treat yourself to a writer's notebook solely for deliberate practice.

I like Moleskines or Leuchtturm notebooks – they're built to last! Or try Ryman in the UK.

Don't buy one so beautiful you're reluctant to use it. So many gorgeous notebooks lie untouched because they're "too nice to scribble in".

Keep it by you when you're reading, or watching TV or film.

Use it to capture techniques you spot in your reading and viewing.

I often flip notebooks and use the two halves in different ways: a scribble half for gathering notes and, flipping it over, a tidy, edited half for future reference.

I use the first page to index later themed pages, such as *time* or *character*. You might prefer to index by authors you're reading, specific genres, or parts of speech such as *verbs*.

Write *Deliberate Practice* on the front, or a title designed to ward off casual readers:

Annual Report Findings. Useful Abbreviations.
Grammar and Punctuation. Advanced Maths.

This is your almanac. Your book of spells. For your eyes only.

How to Use This Book

This book is intended for writers at any stage. You can use it in different ways, depending on your aims.

Writing is a lifelong practice. Like musicians and sportspeople, we're constantly discovering new learning, as writing has so many creative dimensions. I also find that learning resonates differently at different times. Sometimes, I'm not ready for it, or it might seem obvious or superficial. But later on, from a new vantage point and different experience, it falls into place. I'm ready to absorb it.

In the words of the ancient Greek philosopher Heraclitus: "You can't step into the same river twice." Both of you have changed.

I have many dog-eared, well-scribbled writing books that I return to again and again. They bring new impetus each time, as I've changed and grown. Usually, I don't keep reading them for long. They send me straight back to writing. My hope is that you'll find *Deliberate Practice* useful in that way.

I suggest you first quick-scan this book for context. Note anything that jumps out for you, then go back in for close-reading and practice. Don't try to do too much at once. Return later on, from a different place in the river.

Here are some suggestions for ways to approach this book.

Are you new to creative writing study?

If you're new to the idea of studying creative writing, you may find the **Glossary** helpful. It's a quick reference on terminology often used by editors, and on creative writing MFA or MA courses. This offers useful shorthand for discussing writing and narrative technique. Some terms, such as *narrative* and *genre* are in general use, but have a more specific meaning for writers.

I've also included linguistics terms (*verb, noun, pronoun*) which are essential for discussing language at a close-up level.

Most creative writing terminology, especially in fiction and scriptwriting, focuses on what I call "wideshot" concepts: *story, narrative, plot, characterisation, turning-point, viewpoint.* Or larger-scale units: *chapter, oeuvre, voice, novel, poem.*

This scale doesn't handle close reading and writing – the nuts and bolts of what goes on in sentences and paragraphs, word choice, rhythm. For this, you'll find some concepts from linguistics and poetics useful.

But note that deliberate practice doesn't suggest viewing every sentence as a poem, slowing your writing right down, creating heightened effects – unless that's your chosen style. Rather, it's about reading language mindfully, with some detachment as well as enjoyment, so you can discover new tools and effects to develop your writing.

TRY THIS

Pick a topic, such as *time, space, character introductions, beginnings, endings*. Start a new notebook page on this topic, open a book by your favourite author, and gather some examples of how they handle this. This will start to alert you to the *how* of writing.

Do you enjoy self-study courses?

You can use this book as a self-study course tailored to your own interests. Note that it isn't a primer telling you what to do. Rather, it's a recipe for self-learning. It can be used for any genre, style and even language. Use the powerful strategy of deliberate practice to close-read other writers, and develop your own skills and insights.

TRY THIS

Set yourself a month-long or two-week challenge. Pick a daily example from this book, to get up to speed with analytical reading and practice. Then create your own examples to explore writing craft areas you're interested in.

Are you looking for writing inspiration?

For me, the best writing books are the ones I don't finish. Ray Bradbury's *Zen in the Art of Writing*. Margaret Atwood's *Negotiating with the Dead*. So many others.

I don't finish them because they inspire me to start writing.

Feel free to use this book as a kickstart. Dive in, choose a daily writing experiment, and get writing yourself. I would love that!

TRY THIS

Pick a pattern exercise at random from this book as a starting point for freewriting. Or write your own variation on the pattern, and use it as a freewriting prompt.

Interested in exercises and *études*?

Exercises and *études* are proven and effective ways to improve your technique in sports and the arts.

Sports people do "reps" and drills.

Artists make sketches, and copy old masters.

Musicians practise chord progressions, scales, arpeggios, and *études*.

I like the word *étude* (French for "study") because, although *études* are designed for deliberate practice, they're also expressive creative works in their own right. Frédéric Chopin's *Piano Études* are played and performed in concert halls all over the world.

An *étude* for the fiddle might include lots of string crossing, to help violinists to improve their bowing technique. In basketball, you might do form shooting, to develop your muscle memory and improve your accuracy.

This kind of focused, analytical study is the heart of deliberate practice, and you'll find lots of exercises and patterns to try up ahead.

As soon as you're familiar with the principles, make your own examples.

TRY THIS

Choose a short example of writing that moves you, makes you feel something new or intriguing, or illustrates a writing technique you want to try. Examine the writing closely. Break it into parts. Analyse the technique. Practise variations. Then use it in your writing.

Need a kick-start?

I used to find it hard to dive into writing, especially in the early days, when my analytical brain and my creative brain were locked in battle.

So, I used morning pages[9] – also known as freewriting – as a kick-start. Just start writing. Follow the trail of what's on your mind.

For a while, morning pages were helpful. I ended up with pages and pages of stream of consciousness (which I'd die if anyone read), and the occasional glimmer of gold.

But it was mostly unfocused – if cathartic – rubbish. So, I started using random prompts taken from a book. These were more focused, and eventually became a collection of microfiction, *Nanonovels*.[10]

Looking back, it's clear to me that my *Nanonovels* were an example of deliberate practice. I was exploring resistance, and the feeling of writing into the dark, without knowing anything at all about what might turn up. I set a time limit of five minutes for each story, generated a random stimulus, and had to complete some kind of story shape, without edits. Over a hundred days of the experiment, I learned to trust the action of diving in. This was freewriting with a purpose.

I still use freewriting as a warm-up when I need to, but again, with a specific intention.

That might be a deliberate practice exercise, or a focused question about work in progress. *What does my character really want? What might these characters say to shame or inspire each other? What can my character see from their nearest window?*

If you do this just to ease the way in, with no expectation, you'll often find gems on the way. It's a playful way to outwit the editor part of your brain. I find it more productive than random freewriting, and often use it for problem-solving as I write.

TRY THIS

Choose an exercise from this book, and use it as a warm-up. Spend five or ten minutes. No pressure, no obligation, no sharing, no editing. Even if you're not practising a specific language point, this can help with focus, centering, and getting started.

TRY THIS

Write down a question relevant to your work in progress. If you're not sure what to write, ask your character a question. What do you want to know about them? Freewrite for at least ten minutes to surface some answers.

Diagnose writing issues

If you've been writing for a while and worked with an editor, you may have an idea of what areas of craft you need to work on. This kind of professional feedback is gold, even if you find it hard to agree with, accept, or act on.

Even bestselling authors learn and grow, and are open to constructive feedback. Early in his career, the British novelist Louis de Bernières, who wrote *Captain Corelli's Mandolin*[11], was told by his agent that he wasn't very good at creating characters. Undaunted, he said "I'll show you"[12], and went away and worked on his characterisation. If a famous award-winning author can take critical feedback, so can you!

But it can be hard to translate general advice – "*write better characters*" – into *specific actions* for your writing. Characterisation is so multi-dimensional, as people are. A deliberate practice approach can help you to break it down. What does characterisation mean in terms of story? In terms of language? In terms of character motivation? Viewpoint? Voice? Description?

In de Bernières' case, characters in his early novels are described in an abstract way, almost as ciphers. There's a lot of "telling", from a detached viewpoint. Later on, we get to hear from characters' inner lives, but it's still not a fully immersive viewpoint. To me, it feels unmoored, unanchored in physical reality.

But why? What in the actual writing, the words themselves, is contributing to this feeling?

At this point, with deliberate practice, it's time to read as a writer, and dig deep into the language.

Close-read what's going on. What type of words are being used? Verbs, nouns, adjectives? What's the viewpoint? What tenses are being used? How close is the character to what they're experiencing? How close are we as readers? What senses are in play? What do rhythms and idiolect do to help the illusion we're in their shoes?

In de Bernières' later novels, he writes a lot more sensory detail from character viewpoints. This makes them feel much more embodied, more grounded. It also lets the reader see and feel the world around the characters.

He uses different *language*.

It's important to emphasize this, because editors don't often have time to offer specific feedback at the level of language. Or teach you about language, and how it deeply affects the reader's experience.

Deliberate practice can sensitise you to language choices. This might sound a lot of work, given the many dimensions in play, but it's not as much as you think. There are a few key techniques which, once you get to grips with them, will make all the difference to your writing.

What if you don't have editorial feedback to draw on? In that case, find some beta readers online, and ask focused questions. This will be more productive than "*what do you think?*" and "*do you like it?*" types of question. Ideally, you also want specific examples from the writing itself.

Can you see my characters? What helped? What phrases stood out?

Did you gain a vivid sense of place? What helped? What language helped?

Do the action scenes have plenty of pace? What helped? What language held up the action?

Do you care deeply about what happens to the characters? At what point, and why? What language stood out?

Were you confused at any point? Where and why? Can you point out the phrases that confused you?

Don't ask for feedback on a whole novel draft until you've tried shorter excerpts – say, a chapter, or opening paragraphs, and acted on that feedback.

The aim overall is to develop your writing muscles and your toolkit of techniques.

Ready to Get Started?

Five minutes are all you need. Start right now, or pick a time and put it in the diary.

Choose a deliberate practice exercise or pattern (see **Parts 3 and 4**). Deep breath, then just start.

Well, yes – sometimes, this is easier said than done! When I started out, I needed to trick my brain, so you might like to try a few tricks I use. These have evolved over time, as I've got more used to diving in without resistance. It's easier to maintain momentum if you write regularly, but if you only have occasional pockets of writing time, you might find these tricks useful.

Use a timer. This can help you to pull focus. Once you're in the zone, it's easier to keep going. For *Nanonovels*, I used a strawberry-shaped kitchen timer set to just five minutes – a laughably short period.

At other times, I've used a phone app, and the *Pomodoro* Technique, named after the Italian word for "tomato", again inspired by a kitchen timer. A *pomodoro*, for anyone new to it, is a timed period of 25 minutes, followed by a short break.

I started with short periods of writing, but as my focus and momentum improved, pomodoros weren't long enough. I now use time blocks of one or two hours.

I've also tried writing online with experienced writer friends, in a small group. I was unsure at first – would I feel self-conscious?

Do you need the camera on? It turned out that everyone in the group finds it extremely helpful, and gets a lot done. Some prefer the camera on, others off. There's no obligation to share or speak, though we spend a couple of minutes at the start, setting intentions. We've learned a lot from each other's processes and strategies.

Over time, you'll learn what works best for you. In the spirit of B.J. Fogg's *Tiny Habits*,[13] I've found that incremental, experimental change sticks longer than trying to radically change everything at once.

You can also find pockets of time by using your everyday reading as a chance for deliberate practice. Rather than being swept along by your current book, choose a paragraph, read closely, feel how you're reacting, and work out what the writer is doing to achieve those effects.

Keep your notebook handy for capturing examples. Trust me – you won't remember! Actively making notes helps you to clarify your thoughts, and studies have shown it improves retention. Over time, your notebook will become a fantastic reference.

TRY THIS

Think back to times when you managed to focus intently, push distractions aside, and successfully manage a commitment. What factors helped? What were the stakes? Maybe you had to catch a flight? Sit an exam? Take someone to hospital? Or an everyday pressure – it's amazing how much can get done when you have visitors arriving in 20 minutes! Note down your feelings and analyse the factors that helped. Was there a countdown you had to stick to? Were you well prepared? Were you surrounded by other people? What parameters and memories can you draw on to access your best state of intense focus?

TRY THIS

Keep your deliberate practice notebook next to your reading pile. Start a habit of close-reading one paragraph a day, and making notes. Try just five minutes, to start with. If it's possible to write a *nanonovel*, learn French vocabulary, or do some wall push-ups in five minutes, it's possible to do deliberate practice. B.J. Fogg's research shows that it's easier to build habits if you start with tiny, almost effortless commitments, and set up cues or prompts so they're in constant view – the "running shoes by the door" trick. What's the equivalent for your writing?

TRY THIS

Streaks and chains! Keep up momentum by starting either a challenge (*a week, 30 days, 100 days...*), or a streak or chain (*start and keep going*). The US comedian Jerry Seinfeld famously has a "don't break the chain" strategy, where he uses a calendar to note every day that he writes. And he writes every day, without fail. But it can be easy to feel discouraged when you break a streak. A one-time failure can't be allowed to derail your entire streak. Build in a "grace day" to let you off the hook occasionally. I found this concept in an ADHD app, and discovered it's also used in golfing, when it's known as a "mulligan" – a free pass to retake a poor shot without a penalty. It strikes me as a very practical and forgiving way to maintain a habit.

Next Up

The next section is a quick overview of the background theory and foundations of deliberate practice, explaining the steps, and why it works.

If you're in a hurry to get started on *doing* deliberate practice, jump ahead to **Part 3** or **Part 4**, and come back here later.

Part 1

Deliberate Practice Foundations

The Short Feedback Loop

The short feedback loop is the heart of deliberate practice.

It's the key difference between how most aspiring writers approach writing, compared with the practical training I had in the writing professions.

I've always been struck by the contrast between the learning approaches in these two strands of writing.

When I was training as a young journalist, I got feedback *every 100 to 200 words*.

That's right. For every news story I wrote – and these were short items, for spoken broadcast – I got detailed feedback. Every day, I sat with an experienced editor who unpicked every aspect of my writing. Just a paragraph or two of writing. That's a tiny feedback loop.

And at first, I made loads of mistakes. It was tough. Humbling. Hair-raising. And, of course, highly educational.

31

After a while of this tiny feedback loop, I began to see patterns, and could write and edit much more quickly. I also had better understanding of what I was writing about. My confidence and experience grew. I could drop the basic training wheels.

Over time, I needed less and less feedback. It was time to fly solo. Almost.

Because there was always a second pair of eyes – from the desk editor, or another writer. Then came a time when the roles reversed, and I began to check other people's writing. This, too, was useful learning.

Of course, this training was a massive privilege. Not everyone has that chance. But the model itself isn't unusual. It's a classic master-apprentice relationship, familiar to anyone who has learned a craft or trade.

Learning by doing, short feedback loop, experienced mentor.

And in writing and editorial jobs, this isn't unusual.

At one point, I trained on the job as a translator. The approach was exactly the same. First, a short, easy assignment, with detailed feedback from an editor. This feedback went straight into improving the next assignment.

Over time, jobs got longer, more difficult. Always pushing at the edges of my skills. This "pushing at the edges" turns out to be crucial in deliberate practice, as you'll discover.

Maybe deliberate practice is starting to sound more familiar?

Here's another short feedback loop. When I was a kid, I had the chance to learn a musical instrument. These were the days of free school music lessons, so I was incredibly lucky.

Except the instrument picked out was the ton-weight, battle-scarred school cello. A beast of a thing for a small girl. Never mind learn to *play* it – I first had to learn how to *carry* it, not drop the bow, bash my head on the scroll, or jab anyone with the spike in the school corridor – which happened quite often.

If you've played guitar, the process was similar. First, exercises, painfully building finger corns. Then little tunes. Then harder tunes. I got weekly feedback, practised and improved. It gradually got easier. And I had the corns to show for it.

32

What I never did, during all this learning – and this is the crucial bit – was:

> *Attempt to play a whole concert, and then get feedback notes.*

Or:

> *Write an entire news bulletin, and put it on air for feedback.*

Or:

> *Translate a keynote conference speech, and try it in front of the audience.*

And yet, that's how most adults seem to approach writing.

Write a whole draft, then send it out for feedback.

I've met new fiction writers who've written a *whole novel draft* before getting any feedback.

That's 80k words before a single soul sees any writing.

80k words of – to quote Henry James – "a baggy monster"[14] which they then can't face editing.

As a teacher of creative writing, I saw the results of this constantly. It drove me nuts! It's one of the reasons I wrote this book.

I felt people were wasting hours, months and even years on splurge drafts which needed a huge amount of fixing. Whereas by learning some solid craft foundations, they could catch a lot of issues early on.

To me, writing a book has similarities with any other big, long-term project.

If you build a house, you don't first build a wonky house, and then get feedback on how to shore up the collapsing walls, rewire the dodgy electrics, hand-pick grit from the paint and plaster.

More likely, you'd say: That's a *lot* of desnagging. I can't face it. And probably bail out.

I'd certainly find it overwhelming.

With writing, as with houses, there are so many dimensions operating at once. It's hard to know where to start.

In practice, what happens at this point? You might pay for a reader's report. This will typically cover story, style, characterisation, pace, flow, signposting, grammar, punctuation and everything else in one go. And of course, it can be extremely helpful.

But it can only scratch the surface. And you've still got the biggest, gnarliest fixer-upper project on your hands.

Meanwhile, I've spoken to editors and teaching colleagues, and compared what they say with my own experience feeding back on work in progress.

They confirmed what I've long suspected. When they read new writing, they can sense the craft level *instantly*.

The first page already gives a pretty good picture of the writer's stage.

If you're an experienced slush pile reader, you can typically filter out a lot of "passes" – rejections – in just a page or two – though you may well read more, just to make sure.

Decision-making can be quicker than aspiring writers would like. Because if you're an editorial reader and read piles of submissions, you really develop your craft expertise, and your "pass" filter.

You especially develop craft technique if your job involves feeding back to writers, because you have to look into detail of *why* and *what*, and offer solutions.

Of course, now and again, you find an absolute treasure – happy days! You're swept right into the story, in the hands of a skilled, confident storyteller. You read as a *reader*, immersed, engaged, and excited to know what happens next.

More usually, the nagging voice of your diagnostic sixth sense chips in: *Puppeting. Ghost characters. Not enough signposts. Head-hopping. Clunky dialogue…*

Now, these points are relatively straightforward to learn and solve. They're just writing and editing craft.

But if writers get feedback on every issue at once, they'll typically get overwhelmed. After all, they've written 200 more pages without having a handle on these issues. So, the same feedback points crop up time and again.

To me, most writers can save a lot of time and effort by practising some solid techniques early on. Right away, they can put them to work, and write a far better first draft.

You don't need to start with an 80k novel. Try a 2,000-word short story. Or daily microfiction. Very different animals, but a great way to try out techniques, without investing months and years of your life.

So, enough soapbox for now! My hope is that deliberate practice can save you some precious time, and give you better impact from all the time and effort you're putting into your writing.

But hang on, you may be saying. "*Practice*" sounds uncreative. I'm a discovery writer, an experimental writer. Or: I'm writing for fun, not for publication. That's fine. Deliberate practice can help and inspire you, too.

In fact, strong craft skills can release you as a writer and artist. If you're no longer distracted by everyday issues – *viewpoint, tense, anchoring* – you can get immersed in the unfolding story, in painting the vivid pictures in your imagination.

Just as a musician who learns scales can play complex new tunes without thinking.

Strong craft skills can transform your sense of flow in writing, and make you a more confident editor.

Writing Adventures and Experiments

Of course, it's rare to be purely a discovery writer, or entirely a plotter. Most of us have a mix of times when writing is wild and freewheeling, times when it's planned, times when it's painful.

If you're mainly a discovery writer, writing into the dark, going where characters take you, enjoying surprises on the way… great! And if it works for your readers, even better.

I'm still curious about how you handle structure.

Because the structural spadework still has to be done at some point – either by you, in your head or on paper, or by a highly-paid editor.

It's tough to edit a complete discovery draft. It needs cool detachment to do heavy structural lifting, shunt around entire chapters, cut plot strands, kill your darlings, throw out 30k words where the plot ran out of steam, ditch chapters 1-10 because a secondary character took over...

And doing this while you're deep in the flow of words, keeping closeup view and helicopter view in play at the same time.

Deliberate practice of craft can help you to iron out issues you *can* control, and leave breathing space for the fun part – your creativity. In the same way that a movie crew know their kit and skills inside out, freeing them up to respond creatively in the moment.

Deliberate practice is also great for outside-the-box thinking, and creative experiments. Later on, we'll look at techniques such as "cut-up" and "blackout", and the French experimental writers, the *Oulipo* workshop – ideas that can help to cut through block and reenergise your practice.

You might enjoy a fascinating documentary by the maverick Danish director, Lars von Trier: *The Five Obstructions*[15]. On the surface, it's about two leading film directors and the power play between them. But it's really about creative constraints, and how they can refresh your thinking.

Deliberate practice is also super-productive for writers switching from other forms – say, journalists turning to fiction or screenplays. If that's you, you'll want to cut to the chase, identify the craft skills you're lacking, and address those gaps. Probably by close reading some of your favourites, with highlighter pen in hand. That's the essence of deliberate practice.

Whether you're a discovery writer, a plotter, or a writer in another form or genre, experienced or aspiring, deliberate practice will sky-rocket your learning.

And helpfully, it fits in with the writing you already do.

I sometimes turn to deliberate practice as a creative refresh, to problem-solve, or to think outside the box. Always asking: "how can I adapt this? How can I give it my own spin?"

And I'm far from alone. As playwright Simon Stephens says, "Watch and read not like a fan and not like an academic, but like a thief."[16]

Or, if you prefer, like an apprentice learning from a seasoned craftsperson – which is a time-honoured approach in any craft.

Now for a closer look at practice, why it's so powerful, and where it fits with talent.

Nature or Nurture?

Which camp are you in?

Do you believe excellence is in someone's *nature* – an innate golden gift they were born with?

Or does it come from *nurture* – learning, effort, passion and commitment?

Of course, *nature versus nurture* is a false dichotomy. Born talent and learned talent – in any skill – can't be separated. They reinforce and inspire each other.

But still, it's good to examine critically the theory that some people are natural born geniuses in their field, while others get there through learning and practice.

Because one way of thinking is empowering, and the other is profoundly disempowering. And I definitely prefer *empowering*.

Let's look at *nature* first – the idea that people excel because they're a natural born star.

Well, it's true that some people have enormous natural advantages in life. Maybe you're supersensitive to audio and sound pitches, and become a musician. Or have an amazing eye and steady nerves, and try your hand at archery or wildlife photography.

And then, there's your environment, which is immensely important for learning.

We all have *latent* talent for many things – writing, gardening, engineering, leadership. But we become good at *specific* things, in part because of the people and opportunities around us. Mentors, inspirational people, and access to practical equipment.

Bill Gates had a basic computer as a teenager, and spent hours hunkered away, learning how to use it.

The Polgar sisters had a chess-savvy father as their personal trainer.

If you're a keen angler, you might have friends or family who go fishing, and nurture your interest.

If you're a guitarist or drummer, you might have friends to jam with, and tips and musical inspirations to share.

Those extra factors spark your latent interest, and make you keen to learn more. So, it's a self-reinforcing loop.

But maybe you're on your own, with an unusual passion that nobody else in the neighbourhood really gets?

Well, that can be motivational, too. Maybe you have more determination *despite* everyone – precisely *because* you're on your own.

The poet Emily Dickinson was an unconventional recluse whose work was mostly unrecognised in her lifetime. Ray Bradbury was mocked as a child for his love of science fiction and fantasy. The painter Vincent Van Gogh was also marginalised for his uniqueness. The professor of animal science Temple Grandin was misunderstood due to her autism.

Yet all persevered with great passion and became outstanding and influential in their field, despite their uniqueness – or because of it?

Maybe if other people don't helpfully validate you, you just get on with what you love?

Nature and nurture are so complicatedly interwoven with our individual psychologies and situations.

And in the history of education, the emphasis has shifted between nature and nurture, with each dominating at different times, as different research findings and ideologies come through.

During my teacher training in the 1980s/90s, *nurture* was dominant. The thinking was: Excellence isn't simply an innate talent. It can be taught and practised. This learning movement was influenced by the work of psychologist B.F. Skinner[17] on behaviourism.

The focus was on learning through physical actions, rather than just mental states. "Skills and drills", repetition and practice, were the way to go.

If you learned French at the time, you might recall the words *écoutez et répétez* – listen and repeat. I'm a visual learner, so it didn't go well for me.

TRY THIS

Take a moment to think through times when you learned effectively, and when you didn't. What sort of situations? Was it quiet, noisy, calm, busy? Were you on your own, with a coach, or in a classroom? What senses were you using? This will be useful for when you're designing your own unique deliberate practice.

But in time, the pendulum swung in the nature-nurture debate. At the turn of the millennium, influential books such as *The Nurture Assumption* by Judith Rich Harris[18] and *The Blank Slate* by Steven Pinker[19] reasserted a focus on nature.

Harris found that learning was more influenced by genes and peer groups than by the nurture of parents and the home. Pinker emphasized biology, rejecting the idea of humans born as blank slates and created by their cultural surroundings. Nature was back in charge.

However, the pendulum has now swung firmly back to nurture, and the importance of learning and practice. This still holds today. It's a far more more optimistic view, and aligns well with new opportunities for bitesize and individualised learning online.

What led to this change? A big influence on the swing back to nurture was a research paper with the unwieldy title, *The Role of Deliberate Practice in the Acquisition of Expert Performance*. This study by Professor Anders Ericsson[20] looked into what it takes to make an expert. And it might have stayed hidden in academic backwaters, if it hadn't inspired Malcolm Gladwell to write his bestseller, *Outliers: The Story of Success*.[21]

Even if you've not read the book, you've probably come across the *10,000 hours* idea: that to achieve excellence in any field, you need to put in around – well, 10,000 hours.

The catchy number popularised by Gladwell ignited the public imagination. Maybe we can all become superstars, if we put our minds to it?

To me, it sounds both encouraging and impossible, so I've chunked it down to a more manageable concept. It works out at about 20 hours a week, across a decade. Or three hours a day, every day, for ten years.

At this point, intriguingly, 10,000 hours starts to chime with other time and practice concepts: Stephen King's 2,000 words a day, every day. Ray Bradbury's daily writing in the library,[22] a story a week. Ursula LeGuin's daily schedule.[23]

The upshot is: it's about putting the work in.

Of course, 10,000 hours of practice is simplistic. Not everyone who puts the work in achieves excellence.

There was an inevitable backlash. *It's a myth! I've been playing guitar for 40 years and still haven't improved. 10,000 hours will never turn me into a shot-putter – I don't have that physical ability.*

But neither Gladwell nor Ericsson claimed that 10,000 hours of practice is a cast-iron guarantee of success. Ericsson simply uncovered a rough average time that skilled performers took to reach expert level.

And his crucial finding: it's not about the *number* of hours you practice – it's about *how* you spend them. Quality, not quantity. And the key is: *deliberate* practice.

Ericsson's research showed that deliberate practice is a powerful learning strategy for improving performance. He discusses the psychology, the process, and, importantly, practical ways to apply it.

His findings are now a significant element of best practice in education and learning.

Do an online search for "deliberate practice in education", and you'll find thousands of sites where teachers are discussing the topic. Deliberate practice is viewed as the backbone of purposeful, systematic learning.

This makes it a great fit for individualised learning, for self-study, and for people short of time.

So, following on from this groundbreaking research study, what about applications to *writing*?

That's where this book comes in – at the practical, *nurture* end of the spectrum, where you can actively make a difference to your skills. No muses, no myths.

I've already described my experiences in different writing professions, and the apprenticeship model in crafts and trades.

But there are a lot of myths around writing in particular. And for many aspiring authors, the romance of writing is a big part of the attraction.

So many of the literary life stories we love to read are wild, exciting whirlwinds of romance, genius and rock-and-roll habits. If you love this, and find it helps you to write, great.

But if it you're sceptical, it's worth looking into what might lie behind it, and how deliberate practice can help.

The Problem with Genius

As I've said, I find the idea of innate genius problematic and disempowering. So much success is about work and passion meeting opportunity, facilities and your tribe.

For me, the idea of genius mystifies writing, and makes it seem inaccessible.

> *Maybe it's something only geniuses can do? Those people with their names on books on shelves?*
>
> *Maybe you need a mysterious muse to do it at all?*
>
> *Or some kind of epiphany?*

As a book-devouring kid, those are some of the myths I had about writing and writers. And here's another:

> *Maybe you need to do the artist-in-garret thing? Starve yourself, or you're somehow not a real artist?*

If you believe this damaging Romantic nonsense, read *Real Artists Don't Starve* by Jeff Goins.[24]

Before I started writing, it all seemed so mysterious, so out of reach, and not for the likes of me.

But the more I actually did writing as a job, the more I asked: *Who planted those stories?*

Because they *were* stories. If you meet the backstage life of writers, journalists, scriptwriters, they're just like everyone else. And, being honest, far from romantic.

Writing is their job. They show up at the desk. Just as everyone shows up at their workplace.

Yes, there are wonderful inspirational moments and adventures and epiphanies, but they're not your daily bread.

If you wait for those to show up, you won't do much writing.

It's much more empowering to realise that writing is a creative craft and art like any other. What you don't know, you can learn. You can nurture. You can practise.

Another pernicious myth is that you need a Muse.

The Muses were nine Greek goddesses of inspiration, each responsible for a different artform.

There isn't a muse of writing as such. The arts job descriptions were different back then. So, depending on your genre, you might hook up with Calliope (*epic poetry*), Clio (*history*), Erato (*love poetry*), Polyhymnia (*sacred poetry*) Melpomene (*tragic theatre*), Terpsichore (*light verse and dance*), and Thalia (*comedy*). Euterpe was a multiskiller responsible for *music* and *lyric poetry*, and probably suffering from burnout. Poetry was overstaffed with three subgenres. And there's an unlikely wildcard among the nine – Urania, the muse of *astronomy*.

Later writers famous for having a Muse in their lives include Dante and his platonic love Beatrice; F. Scott Fitzgerald and Zelda; Virginia Woolf and Vita Sackville-West.

To me, this sounds like a lot of responsibility for the muse. Being so idealised could get wearing. What if you have a sulky off-day and disrupt your mus-ee's concentration? Maybe jeopardize their entire draft?

And what exactly is your role? Keeping the dishevelled, chaotic artist fed and watered? Beta reader? Making sure they do the work – a human pomodoro?

Plus, what's the benefit to you? You may be a gifted artist or writer in your own right. But you'll forever be the "plus one" to the star.

And for the writer, it's an abdication of responsibility. Which may be exactly what you want – but *really*?

That said, I do believe in inspiration, and sudden flashes of insight. I suspect it has a lot to do with brain chemistry and having new experiences to feed your creative well. Reading, travel, conversations, books, people and moments that come into our lives – they're all gifts that help us to grow.

And if it helps to attribute these gifts to a muse or supernatural being, why not? Get creative!

Just don't leave your writing inspiration in the hands of a capricious Muse. It's giving them far too much power. In fact, giving a muse a capital letter is giving them too much power.

So, don't wait around for a muse to show up. Make time in your diary, commit to it, and start. Keep starting. Inspiration will appear.

By the way, I have a theory about who benefits from those writer myths. On the one hand, the publishing industry. On the other, writers themselves. After all, if you make writing seem difficult and mysterious, then you'll seem glamorous and amazing, sell books, and put off the competition.

It's just a theory. Don't waste time wondering. Get on with writing.

TRY THIS

Invent your own muse. Think back to people who have inspired you in the past. Who lights up your life and gets you excited? Who challenges you with their incisive views and new knowledge? Who is a stern, wise critic who takes no nonsense and sets high standards? Who is way ahead of you on a similar path and is someone to look up to? Who makes you feel strong and alive as a creator? Brainstorm your ideal attributes, fuse them into a character, and have a conversation with them. You might start by asking *questions: "What do you want to tell me?" "What do you see as my biggest challenge?"* and writing what they tell you.

TRY THIS

Consider the opposite of your ideal muse – your anti-muse. What sort of attributes do they have? What experiences have felt to you like an anti-muse? Brainstorm what you find. What can you learn from this about your needs? What relationships and experiences help you to thrive, and what makes your creativity wither? If you consider the anti-muse as a character, how might you transform them into writing gold, and loosen their power?

TRY THIS

Set up an invisible committee of mentors. You have an unlimited budget, so choose the best. The people can be real or fictional, close family, media stars, historical figures. They don't have to be friendly, or patient – any committee needs a mix of skills and viewpoints. Crucially, they're all on your side. You might like to look into Carl Jung's archetypes to discover more about the internalised mentor figures we all share, or draw on a mix of modern and older archetypes: *the Sage, the Critical Friend, the Healer, the Rebel, the Trickster, the Innovator.*

Writing by Osmosis

Formal training for writers is patchy at best. Osmosis – natural absorption – is the usual way. Again, I find this problematic. Let's look at typical paths into writing, and where the gaps are.

Most people learn their writing skills in two phases: early writing training at school, and some further learning as an adult.

As an adult learner, you have a whole different set of skills and questions. You've seen more of life, so you have far better learning strategies. You probably want to cut to the chase – which is a great fit for deliberate practice.

But mostly, we get our writing training at school, for a few brief years. And then it stops dead.

Wow! Imagine a guitarist learning a few songs at school, and that's it. Never getting lessons, never learning new techniques, improving your skills, studying other players.

Imagine a boxer deciding that school training is enough. Never seeking out an adult training gym, coach or mentor. Dangerous, or what?

But writers somehow view things differently. We devour books, TV and movies, listen to people speaking, and pick up writing skills and stories that way.

Well, yes, to a degree. I call this the "osmosis" theory of writing. But translate that into another artform: the guitarist who listens to loads of records; the boxer who watches endless matches on TV.

I may be wrong, but this sounds suspiciously like armchair wrestling, or backseat driving. Yes, you're absorbing a lot. But you're looking on at it.

Deliberate practice is far more active and involved.

I find that writers often miss the *practice* step. There seems to be an unspoken idea that because you can speak, you can write. Because you can write emails and work documents, you can write novels and short stories.

To me, that's a problem. School writing skills aren't enough, or advanced enough, to bridge the gap to professional adult writing. Why would they be? We don't expect junior or high school tech skills to qualify you as a professional engineer.

Plus, at school, you're taught in big classrooms. It's noisy. Everyone has different needs. It's hard to go deep.

If you miss school due to illness or upheavals, you can easily get behind, with long-term repercussions. Whereas good foundations have a "compound interest" effect. You're off and running, you catch the reading and writing bug, and *then* you can learn by osmosis.

During my research, I've been interested to see educators describing writing as "caught, not taught".

The thinking is that mostly, we "catch" writing as it flies by. If you're lucky, you'll grab it, get infected with passion for reading and writing. You'll become a voracious reader, and you'll pick up a good ear and style by absorbing patterns from your reading.

But if you don't catch writing, you'll miss that moment. It's gone.

To me, that's classic osmosis learning. It's a very hit-and-miss approach for such a crucial skill. And that's most people's experience.

But surely after our school days, things improve? Surely writing training doesn't stop dead? What about writing training at college? And I'm not talking about specialist creative writing degrees here. Most writers don't have that chance.

Did you ever get training at college? Or feedback on your writing?

I didn't. On content of essays, yes. On writing itself, never. Again, there was an osmosis approach: read a lot, and absorb style and craft as a by-product.

There was an assumption that you didn't need to actively learn.

And yet, at that time of life, students are hungry, learning and blossoming in every other walk of life.

Kids into music and sports are deep in serious one-to-one coaching, and storming ahead with their ambitions.

You, as a writer? Training? Not so much.

So, what about the next stage – the world of work. On your first job, did you ever get writing training? Feedback on your writing?

Maybe a few people correcting your typos. Or pointing you towards Grammarly. Which corrects bloopers – great! – but again, doesn't teach you how to write.

In short, most people have had little or no writing training since school.

But secretly, we dream of writing a novel.

And one day, the writing bug bites, the muse strikes, and we sit down and write it. Maybe 50k words, with support and comradeship from the fabulous *NaNoWriMo*[25] writing initiative. Then on to 80k words. The first draft.

Which is a huge, fantastic achievement.

But without any training, what's the chances we're nailing the craft?

This might sound concerning. But it's actually very exciting, and encouraging. This gap can be addressed very effectively, through deliberate practice.

Deliberate practice is great for adult learners short on time.

Before we get down to the brass tacks of practical application, I'd like to share two parallel writer stories, comparing the learning journeys of Mel, a first-time novelist, and Skye, a trainee journalist.

A Writer's Tale – Mel

Mel, the aspiring novelist, wants to write a thriller. She loves thrillers and devours them: whether books, TV series or films.

So, she sits down and starts writing – let's say, during National Novel Writing Month, *NaNoWriMo*, in November.

She toughs out writing 50k words – fantastic! A first draft.

She spends a couple of months editing and expanding it to 80k.

She sends it to a publisher in London or New York. They snap it up as part of a three-book deal and her life is made.

Sorry, that didn't happen.

She researches some publishers and sends the book out. Waits months. It comes back. Rejection. *Not for us.*

Some promising feedback, though. The book needs more work. So, she hires a professional editor.

It turns out there are lots of different kinds of editor.

She hires a proofreader. The job takes many hours, and costs a lot. And to be honest, the proofreading has only tidied things up. No structural edits, no real line wrangling to improve her craft.

Out goes the book. Comes back. Several times.

This process takes *a couple of years*. Meanwhile, Mel is hard at work on the next book.

It's taking a long time to find a publisher for the first one.

She decides to self-publish. Some writers are doing incredibly well in this area. Plus, it will give her control of the process and timelines.

It takes a few months to learn self-publishing. The book is published and sells a few copies online. Not enough to recoup all the hours spent. But enough to keep hopes alive.

And the years pass. And pass. A few books sold. Hopes still alive.

Mel has put in extraordinary time, effort and cost, often for years. Yet she has never learned writing craft.

Yes, she's spent months, years of her life *writing*. Her first novel was 80k words.

Her second is even longer, at 120k. And her third is looking like 150k.

That's a lot of writing.

But very little feedback, in all that time.

A Writer's Tale – Skye

Meanwhile, Skye is a trainee writer in the writing industries, getting one-to-one editorial feedback from an experienced colleague.

Learning on the job. A sink-or-swim scenario.

There are a *lot* of edits.

Coming in as a college-fresh know-it-all, Skye finds this painful. Ego defences are on high alert. But learning loads about concision, clarity, style and, bizarrely, confidence. So, it's all worthwhile.

The feedback loop at this early point is short – maybe 200-1,000 words.

Skye pitches a script to a new writing scheme and amazingly, gets a first commission.

Time for more on-the-job feedback – long phone calls with a script editor.

A great idea, vivid, clear writing voice and crackling dialogue skills are taken as read.

This feedback is about structure and clarity, and has longer feedback loops. The editor asks questions that expose woolly thinking. This helps Skye to address character motivation, pace, plot holes, boring scenes and anything overwritten.

The notes have to be turned round in a week. Skye learns to write and edit faster, more robustly – and be less precious with words.

Skye starts to write romance novels. They love the genre, have a lively, distinctive voice, and spend a good while studying other writers' style and structure. They find a publisher.

For their first book, they're paired with a line editor for rigorous one-to-one training in fiction techniques.

This takes their writing to a new level of professionalism. Skye now writes several books a year. And isn't a native speaker of English.

These are real scenarios from people I know in different writing professions. The point is that professional writers welcome and thrive on editorial advice, learning and feedback. Getting pages of notes and pointers on where you're going wrong doesn't mean you're a terrible writer, an embarrassing fail.

On the contrary, it's a gift that means you show great promise, and you're worth investing time in.

But do you really need to do the undeniable work of learning the craft of writing? First, ask yourself...

What's Your Motivation?

If you're perfectly happy with your writing, don't change a thing.

If you're enjoying it, and getting the results you want – whatever your definition of success – then it's working for you.

Many writers are where they want to be.

With just enough validation, sales, creativity and writing friends to fulfil them. They don't need to go beyond their comfort zone. If that's you, embrace it.

It's a beautiful place to be. Not everyone who sings a song wants to train as a singer. Not everyone who enjoys playing football wants to join an ambitious team.

Maybe you just want to get your book out there, as a legacy for family and friends. Or just have fun. Let yourself off the hook!

But if you're keen to grow, learn craft, and level up your skills, deliberate practice is for you. Close reading, analysis and experimenting is a super-effective way to improve your writing and understand how writers achieve their effects.

Over time, you'll get your eye and ear in, see patterns and rhythms, and be able to edit much more quickly and confidently.

You'll also learn the concepts and terminology you need to work professionally with editors.

So, it's well worth committing a short amount of time to practice.

Growth Mindset

One obstacle to growth is that your body and mind don't make it easy to learn anything new – literally. We have a deep-rooted physical and psychological response to challenges.

With new situations, our adrenaline kicks in – the fear chemical. It puts our senses on high alert. Familiar situations, meanwhile, feel safe and comfortable – chemicals such as oxytocin flood our bodies. That's our good old mammal physiology and psychology, and there's nothing much we can do about it.

That said, we *can* challenge these instinctive reactions, and change them, and I'll share some tactics for this shortly.

But first, it's important to realise that this apparent difficulty is an *essential* part of learning. If you don't feel it, you're not in the active learning zone. If you've done sport, you'll be familiar with the idea of *eustress* or "good stress". If you aren't in that zone, you aren't stretching your body. It's similar with learning.

If you're learning something new, at the outer edges of your skill, in the eustress zone, it will trigger a physiological response that feels like fear or anxiety. Writers usually call this "resistance", or "block". Our bodies and minds create sensations of anxiety, to get us to return to "safe and comfortable".

But if we stay in safe and comfortable, we don't progress.

Resistance is a kind of mild pain, like a tiny electric shock, designed to get us back to the easy life. It'll trip you up at every turn, if you don't learn tactics to deal with it. Especially if you want to learn fast.

So, facing down those feelings is vital.

Steven Pressfield has a terrific book on resistance: *The War of Art*.[26] I highly recommend it if (like many of us) you sometimes struggle with inner resistance. It's mainly about ego defence and comfort zones, and how too much comfort stops you from growing.

Deliberate practice is a great tactic for overcoming resistance. It doesn't involve high stakes or deadlines – just playful experiment and doing. It lets you *do* the thing, without fear of failure, rejection, or any of the other bogeymen that crowd our thoughts.

The more you practise, the more you establish a habit. *New* becomes familiar and habitual. And once it's a habit, it's so much easier to get going.

Think back to learning to type, or drive, play a sport, or cook a meal. At first, you feel at sea. Every step needs careful thought. Your body feels gangly and useless, and doesn't do what you want it to.

After some practice, muscle memory kicks in. It's almost hard to imagine a time when you couldn't *do the thing*.

At the same time, something similar happens in your brain. And it's just as physical.

Your brain is made up of billions of nerve cells known as "neurons". These communicate with each other through connectors called "synapses".

When you perform an action, *or think* in a certain way, the relevant neurons fire in a pattern, creating a pathway in your brain. Repetition strengthens the pathway, adding a substance called myelin, which acts a bit like electrician's insulation tape.

The more you repeat something, the more that pathway is insulated and strengthened. Your brain has "wired" the behaviour. It becomes automatic. You've created a habit – something you do almost without thinking.

For me, this realisation about physical wiring in the brain is a gamechanger. It helps to explain why people might shy away from new learning, and feel resistance.

It also addresses questions about the balance between craft and creativity. In order to deal with everyday sensory and cognitive overwhelm, our brain creates shortcuts and patterns.

That's not just a clever, time-saving thing to do. It's how we cope and get oriented in life. Not everything we do can be new, novel and unique all the time. If that were the case, life would be exhausting and impossible.[27]

Deliberate practice can make some writing skills second nature, and free up space for creative flow.

Learning solid craft puts our focus on creativity, rather than everyday problem-solving.

And at the very least, turning some skills into well-honed, habitual craft, rather than the outer edge of new creativity, means you have more tools and tactics at hand to switch in when you need them. Maybe different ways with dialogue. Or tactics for starting a scene. Or ways to move the story forward quickly in time.

Any skill you can shift into a habit rather than brand new learning will make it far easier to write.

Face Down Resistance

Resistance can be personal and emotional – after all, it's a kind of fear. A fear of the unknown, a fear of starting, a fear of failure, a fear of thresholds… in German, there's even a unique word for "fear of thresholds": *Schwellenangst*, which makes it sound even more terrifying, and paints a great picture of a quivering writer at a fearsome portal.

But knowing that's all it is – a chemical feeling from your wonderful brain – can be a great help.

The best antidote to resistance I've ever found is really simple:

JUST START.

It's amazing how just setting a time, sitting down, and getting on with it shatters the imaginary deadlock in your mind.

I've had great success doing this with other writers in an online Zoom group where we all say hello, say what we're doing in the next two hours, and *just start*.

The feeling of camaraderie and accountability really helps.

Try *just start* for a few days in a row. And give yourself freedom to be really terrible.

It should start your creative wheels turning again.

If you don't know where to start, try deliberate practice.

And when facing down resistance, keep in mind a wonderful quote from the TV series *Doctor Who*, spoken by The Eleventh Doctor, played by Peter Capaldi.

> *"Scared is a superpower."* [28]

Anxiety and excitement are chemically the same thing. And adrenaline is a superdrug, helping you to *"run faster, fight harder, jump higher than ever in your life."*[29]

It's true. Adrenaline is the fight-or-flight chemical. It's what you feel coursing through your veins in emergencies, in car accidents, when a plane lurches in a storm. In an instant, it narrows your focus, makes time slow down, sends all your energy towards survival. It's why people *in extremis* can sometimes pull of extraordinary feats of strength, speed or instinct.

TRY THIS

Adrenaline isn't just the fear chemical – it's also the excitement chemical. Try listening in to the voice of your resistance. If you like, give it a recognisable face – maybe a gremlin or Gollum? What's it saying? What kind of cranky, sulky, whiny excuses is it coming up with? Turn it down. Somewhere behind it, there's a voice of excitement in disguise. See if you can tune into it, turn it up. What's it saying? If you like, give the voice a face – maybe you as a young child, or an excitable character from a film. Carry them around with you, and encourage that voice. Writing is an adventure, and you're

the intrepid adventurer. If it doesn't feel exciting, at least some of
the time, maybe you'll find something else more rewarding!

Another useful tactic comes from the books of David Goggins,[30]
an extraordinary Navy SEAL and ultramarathon runner. Goggins
is renowned for putting himself through extreme challenges,
outwitting his internal voices of resistance.

In his view, safe, comfortable choices are obstacles to personal
growth. Goggins deliberately puts himself in uncomfortable
situations to "callous the mind" and build mental toughness.
He sees discomfort for what it can teach him, welcomes it and
seeks it out.

And let's face it, any perceived discomfort of writing pales into
insignificance compared with Goggins climbing a frozen mountain
in the dark with bleeding feet.

Maybe closer to home for writers, the memoir *What I Talk About
When I Talk About Running*,[31] by the Japanese novelist Haruki
Murakami, has some similar thinking. Murakami draws parallels
between his writing and long-distance running, which he does not
just to keep fit, but as a deliberate physical and mental practice.
Murakami has embraced running to build the discipline, resilience,
routine, and perseverance needed for writing, to give space for
meditative thinking, and to help him push beyond his limits.

Of course, maybe this isn't you. It isn't me, either! But I do find
the *extreme* version of deliberate practice helps to put small writing
challenges into perspective. You can easily practise techniques for
dialogue, temporal patterns, active verbs. It's easily doable.

Working on a resistance mindset shift will turn out to be very
useful when it comes to something it's impossible to avoid as a writer:

Resistance to Feedback

Just when you've overcome your inner resistance and written your
novel draft, you might come up against a new kind of resistance:
resistance to feedback.

Writing without feedback is staying in the comfort zone. You won't progress. But comfort is – well, *comfortable*.

Without feedback, your ego is protected. You won't get defensive and feel fear.

You can enjoy the lovely vibe of creating, without the need to think about readers, audience, and the job of editing.

But to progress, you need to get used to feedback from other people – peer readers, editors, critics, friends and family. And it may be critical.

This can be a shock, especially early on your journey. Some writers never recover from their first encounters with feedback. It's not surprising!

Once again, our mammal bodies are throwing a curve ball. Humans are wired to respond to threats more than to positives. So, anything threatening to our egos is naturally more salient, more memorable, than even the most glowing compliments.

As a result, we typically get stuck on the painful comments, and overlook the compliments. And since we usually work alone, it's harder to find positive validation to soothe our battered defences.

Be reassured that this tendency is normal. Once again, reframing can help. It's just growing pains. The gift of learning. A fierce challenge. A rite of passage on the professional ladder.

And for perspective, it's worth knowing that in the professional writing world, feedback can be really direct, incisive, and tough. You might get feedback in a room full of actors. Or at the newsdesk, with a minute till the bulletin goes out. You don't have time to nurse your feelings. You just have to get on with the job.

And that's without even considering the trollfest out there on the internet.

So, there's no way round the feeling of unwelcome feedback. You might not agree with it, but using some of your tactics, and learning what you can from it, will get you to a higher standard more quickly. And this learning is yours for the rest of your writing, for the rest of your life.

Here's more good news.

It's easy to talk about "learning your craft" without considering what that actually means. What's writing craft? Isn't learning endless (yes)? What's *your* craft? Isn't it highly individual (yes)? How do you know you have enough writing craft to embark on that novel (you don't know – you just start).

But here's what I've found teaching hundreds of writers in my teaching work.

The same handful of issues come up time and time again.

Although all writers are very different, there are some typical feedback areas that recur: signposting, faceless characters, puppeting, veering viewpoint, abstraction, and many others.

Your writing has a unique pattern or fingerprint. It's so unique that it's possible to detect your authorship from even a small sample – to the extent that text diagnosis is used to solve crimes, identify the author behind the pseudonym Robert Galbraith[32], or work out which bits of Shakespeare's plays were written by Shakespeare.[33]

So, you're unique, and it's possible to diagnose what combination of learning will help you specifically, and suggest what to practise.

Experienced editors will tell you the same: certain craft issues crop up all the time. Rather than them editing it countless times, it's far more effective to explain the issue to you, so you can learn, and do the edits yourself.

Just as a sports coach or music teacher might diagnose an issue, and prescribe a particular exercise. It's not their job to do it for you.

Every writer has strengths and weaknesses, and tailored feedback on your own writing issues will get you further, faster than generic advice on "how to write".

That's where deliberate practice comes into its own. And it boils down to three simple steps:

IDENTIFY THE ISSUE.
CREATE A SHORT FEEDBACK LOOP.
PRACTISE.

With that, it's time to move on to the background and practicalities of deliberate practice.

Part 2

Deliberate Practice Today

Deliberate practice really hit the mainstream on the publication of Malcolm Gladwell's book, *Outliers: The Story of Success*.[34]

The *10,000 hours* idea – that it takes 10,000 hours of practice to master a skill – is common currency now. But few people dive into the original research by the Swedish psychologist, Anders Ericsson[35]. His work on human excellence and mastery in subjects including chess, music, sports and medicine has been tremendously influential.

And as you know, it's not about the *number* of hours. It's about *how* you spend them.

10,000 hours of mindless repetition won't take you far. It's the *quality* of the practice, not the *quantity*, that counts. The *deliberate* part of deliberate practice.

Ericsson's research showed that *deliberate* practice helped people to improve their skills much faster and more effectively than **unfocused** effort over the same period. It got results.

So, it's time for a look about how deliberate practice works, and how these findings might be applied to writing.

Ericsson's Theory of Deliberate Practice

Ericsson's research proposes that effective practice needs three steps:

BREAK THE ACTION DOWN AND
ISOLATE A **TINY** ELEMENT.

CHOOSE AN ELEMENT JUST
OUTSIDE YOUR COMFORT ZONE.

REPEAT THE ELEMENT AND SEEK
FEEDBACK AS YOU GO.

These three steps are the foundations of deliberate practice, so let's go deeper.

1. Isolate a tiny element

If you play sport or music, this will be familiar.

Let's say you've identified a bug in your technique. A part of the music or an area of gameplay that lets you down.

Maybe your handgrip on your bat or racquet is slightly wrong. Or if you're a musician, you struggle to shift between two positions.

So, you break the problem down. Isolate one tiny section. Maybe a movement from A to B.

You do the movement very slowly, looking at it closely. What exactly is going on here? Where's the problem?

Is it the wrist or the fingers? What's leading the movement? Where's the weakness?

If you can, you get some guidance from a coach or teacher.

Then, you isolate and practise that one shift really slowly.

Feel the individual parts of the motion. It's strange and uncomfortable at first. You're doing something in a new way. You're exercising specific muscles and creating new neural pathways in your brain.

Then, repeat. Over time, you can pick up speed, and the movement becomes embodied and natural. Part of your muscle memory.

And finally, you don't need to think about it. You just do it. You can manage that tricky *barré* chord on the guitar. A low tackle in rugby. The gooseneck technique in basketball.

Of course, writing isn't as physical as sport or music. It's more cognitive – like chess. And your brain isn't a muscle – it's an organ, like your heart or lungs.

But writing does have a physical aspect. And thinking of the brain as a muscle is a useful metaphor for the idea of neuroplasticity – your brain's capacity to constantly learn and evolve.

And language is full of patterns, shapes and structures that can be learned and practised, including flows and rhythms that can be felt physically, as well as emotionally.

Children feel this physical sense of rhythm intuitively when absorbing nursery rhymes and songs. Listen to the beat of *Mary had a little lamb, its fleece was white as snow*. Or *hickory dickory dock, the mouse ran up the clock*.

Actors often find it easier to learn their lines together with movements, linking muscle and spatial memory together with language.

Prose writing and dialogue may be less rhythmic than songs and rhymes, but are still full of patterns and arcs of meaning that create a feeling of flow.

To take a simple example: *on the one hand* – a rising phrase – is usually followed by *on the other hand* – a falling phrase.

On the one hand, I'd love to go to the party. *On the other hand*, I've got too many other commitments.

On the one hand… on the other hand is a common language shape with a rise and fall, or arc.

Other familiar shapes include *question and answer,* and *call and refrain.*

Language shapes and patterns exist along many different dimensions, some of them highly sophisticated. All writers have their own patterns and techniques. And they can be broken down and studied to learn about their impact – emotional, physical, and semantic.

That close analysis is the first concept in Ericsson's idea of deliberate practice. Choose a small, bitesize element.

So, now for Ericsson's second concept:

2. Something outside your comfort zone

A chosen bite for deliberate practice needs to be just at the *edge* of your comfort zone.

Something *slightly* new and needing some thought, but not *too* difficult. A small amount of *eustress*.

Eustress, in contrast to *distress* or "bad stress", is the good stress you need to build your skills, as you'll know if you do sports. If you put your muscles under a slight degree of stress, tearing the fibres just a little, they can then do the mending and thickening that makes them stronger.

Eustress, at the edge of the comfort zone, is where you grow. Where optimum learning takes place. And the sweet spot for deliberate practice.

As an example, here's how it works with someone learning the accordion.

When my partner started to learn, he always started at the beginning of his current practice piece, and played through till he hit a snag. Then he restarted from the beginning, taking another run at it. Always hitting the same snag.

I was taught a different approach: break it down, and practice each tiny chunk, over and over. Then put them together in bigger sections.

I began to wonder why the "take another run at it" approach was ineffective.

It's because you can already play the easy bits. You're wasting time repeating those, when you actually need to sort out the sticking point that's holding back the rest – the weak link.

You won't solve that by bashing through and hoping for the best. Because you don't know how to play the difficult bit.

You're not slowing down, analysing the issue, breaking it into steps. You're just hoping it'll sort *itself* out, over time.

If music is just gentle leisure fun for you, and you have no aspirations to improve, that's fine.

But if you want to improve, you need to tackle issues just beyond the edge of your comfort zone.

Not *too* far outside. If you overreach, you'll try it a few times, get frustrated, bored, and annoyed, then give up.

Whereas if you pick a small challenge, just a small stretch, you'll be in the zone of *eustress*.

So, the idea in deliberate practice is to pick a small *eustress* challenge. It will be slightly uncomfortable at first – and that's the point. That's active learning.

Now on to Ericsson's third concept.

3. Repeat the element

If you've ever joined a gym, you'll be familiar with "reps". They're used a lot in muscle building: 10 reps, take a rest, another 10 reps, and so on.

Repetition doesn't just build physical skills by strengthening muscles; it also builds what's known as *muscle memory*, which is actually a function of the brain. Repetition changes your brain and thought processes by changing neural pathways. In other words, you really can rewire your brain. For more on this, see the overview of Ericsson's *Peak* in **Part 8: The Science of Excellence**.

Repetition for musicians and creative artists goes under different names: *warm-ups, exercises, scales, chords, sketches, drills*. Creativity and habit often go hand in hand.

The role of repetition in the arts sometimes surprises people outside the creative world. There's a fascinating exploration in *The Creative Habit*,[36] by the choreographer Twyla Tharp.

As she explains, routine is essential to her dance practice. She goes to her dance studio at the same time every day. She cuts out all distractions. She's as focused and devoted as the most ascetic monk.

And she's one of the world's foremost *creative* minds.

In all these areas, the aim of deliberate practice repetition is to practise until the new technique stops being slightly uncomfortable *eustress*, gets embodied as second nature, becomes part of your comfort zone, and possibly a habit.

There are different opinions on how long it takes to form a habit. One influential study[37] suggests it can take an average of 66 days.

That's oddly specific and, in fact, the time range in the research study was from around 20 to 250 days. This wide time range depended on individuals, and the complexity of the behaviour. It's much easier to establish a simple habit of drinking a daily glass of water in the morning than of, say, daily exercise that involves more effort, thought and time commitment.

But a key finding was the importance of consistency. Creating a consistent context really helps habits to stick. For a writer, this might mean writing at the same time each day, or at the same desk, perhaps using familiar stationery, or similar comfortable clothes.

Choices like this help to simplify the elements of learning and reduce cognitive load, freeing up your brain's resources. This helps to make the neural pathways stronger and more efficient. Consistency also helps to create triggers that can reinforce the habit – for example, sitting on that seat is your cue for writing. For more on how to harness the natural way people can form habits, see the section on B.J. Fogg's *Tiny Habits*[38] in **Part 8**.

When it comes to feedback, you don't need an expert on hand at every step of the way. You're a reader, as well as a writer. Your own instincts and experiments will tell you if a technique is effective, interesting or productive for you. It depends entirely on what you're aiming for in your writing.

For example, I heard from an experienced student writer who was working on a novel, and tried the Shakespeare and King techniques above. Shakespeare unlocked a way to introduce other characters through a secondary character viewpoint, rather than writing from third person viewpoint. King's technique provided a way to sketch in secondary characters without slowing up action, framed within the main character viewpoint.

The writer understood immersive viewpoint and found that using these techniques brought the action closer. With your reader hat on, you don't need to know or understand the techniques at all – *you'll feel it in the writing.*

Reading your own work calls for a degree of standing back, and seeing with fresh eyes. You need to learn to do this, as an editor of your own work. This, too, can be practised. The techniques I find most useful are coming to it fresh next day, and taking a run at it from further back in the writing. Writing and reading happen at different paces, so you need to simulate an experience of detachment from the super close-up view.

With deliberate practice, you can do short experiments to see the effect, without making wholesale changes or going down a long, winding rabbit hole.

Say you're wondering about changing your novel viewpoint from third person to first, or maybe to free indirect style. Don't just read up on the pros and cons of each. Read some examples, and do an experiment. Change just a paragraph or two. If you like the effect, try a longer section. See how it makes you feel about the world and the character.

The novelist Franz Kafka initially wrote parts of *The Trial*[39] in the first person, and later changed them into third, turning his first person viewpoint into the alienated character of K. Experimenting with language is part of the writing process – and you're in good company!

What's Your Creative Style?

Knowing the basics of deliberate practice and habit formation, you can now start to actively explore and discover what *does* work for you – not by throwing yourself into a full-length novel and writing for eight hours a day, but by doing small experiments.

And you can use deliberate practice to develop not just your writing technique, but also your process.

Because writers are vastly different people in different situations, we all have different ways of working. There's no one-size-fits-all approach or magic key to learning to write. It's highly likely that the creative process that works for Twyla Tharp or Kurt Vonnegut won't work for you.

People also have different learning styles and preferences. I didn't become fully aware of this until well into adulthood. It made such a difference to find out that I was a visual learner, and couldn't for the life of me learn a new language just by listening. I used this discovery to go back to whiteboards and paper processes, which I find more effective than keeping information inside a computer file, where it can get forgotten.

Time spent learning about your own habits and preferences is well spent.

TRY THIS

To get clues about your learning style, think back to what worked for you – or didn't – at school. Think about your approach to building flatpack furniture, or setting up a new digital device. Do you read the manual? Do you rip open the box and get hands-on? Do you give it a go, and look for help when you get stuck? Who do you call on? Each approach is valid, but what can you discover about your own natural affinities? If you're a visual learner, decide on some tools and strategies to help keep you on track, and see **Part 7: Writing Visualisation**. If you're auditory or tactile, consider your writing environment and what puts you in the right frame of mind, whether music or silence, comfortable or office clothes, low distraction, or lots of energising bustle.

As a writing teacher, as well as different learning styles, I've discovered three main approaches to writing a project for publication, based on the writer's psychological preferences. Do any of these seem familiar?

ANALYTICAL – INTERESTED IN
PLANNING AND STRUCTURE

MEDITATIVE – REFLECTING,
SHAPING AS YOU WRITE

EXPLORATORY - DRAFTING WITH SPONTANEITY, REFINING LATER

Or maybe you're a balance of all three?

Each style or preference can benefit from deliberate practice in different ways. Let's break it down.

Analytical creatives include plotters, and writers who devour craft books on structure and form. You may have a systematic or design type of mind.

Many famous and prolific writers have an analytical bent, including writers well before the era of computers. Kurt Vonnegut gave a lecture, *The Shapes of Stories*,[40] where he suggested that

> *"...stories have shapes which can be drawn on graph paper, and ... your brain consists of ever-evolving neurons that can form new connections, and your mind is a learning machine. The shape of a given society's stories is at least as interesting as the shape of its pots or spearheads."*

Vonnegut's theory was submitted as his master's thesis in anthropology to the University of Chicago. It was rejected. But his self-styled "scientific thinking" is remarkably similar to work by screenwriting gurus such as Syd Field and Robert McKee, and more recent discoveries in linguistics-based books, such as *The Bestseller Code*, by Matthew Jockers and Jodie Archer.[41]

Meditative creative writers are more likely to see their writing as reflective practice that's fulfilling in its own right. You may do regular morning pages, free writing, or writing meditations without the pressure of completion.

Thinkers and teachers in this area include Julia Cameron, who pioneered morning pages, Ann Lamott, author of *Bird by Bird*,[42] and Natalie Goldberg, author of *Writing Down the Bones*.[43]

Virginia Woolf, the groundbreaking modernist and author of *Orlando*[44], was another meditative writer who used journaling as a reflective practice.

With this style, deliberate practice can be used to surface new material (try journaling, random stimuli or *Nanonovels*), or work through problems (frame a question for your freewrites). Morning pages needn't be just a warm-up. You can equally choose a specific focus, and take some time afterwards, to read what you've written.

When I tried morning pages, they turned into masses of scribbled paper that I was too overwhelmed to go back to. But in future, I'd use a highlighter to mark up anything striking, to make it easier to mine for scraps of gold whenever I need inspiration.

Exploratory writers or "discovery writers" prefer to follow their instincts and surprise themselves, as well as their readers. This style is sometimes known as "writing into the dark".

Writers known for writing without a clear plan include Stephen King, Margaret Atwood and Neil Gaiman – so once again, you're in great company.

If you're just starting out, this style can seem both liberating and daunting. Some writers are natural storytellers; others struggle with sprawling plotlines which will need big structural edits later.

If that's you, try using deliberate practice as a way to build story skills in a short form, such as microfiction. Try micro-experiments with techniques such as reversals, thumbnail descriptions, or signposts. How can you evoke a brand new world in a few words? How can you shift viewpoint? Novels and short fiction are very different forms, but share similar techniques. Short forms let you experiment and speed up your learning about structure more quickly.

All writers

Whatever your creative style, you're interested in new ideas, stories and concepts.

Deliberate practice isn't just great for craft techniques and problem-solving – it can also be used to energise your writing in different ways.

You might set yourself a reading challenge, as Ray Bradbury suggests[45] – "a poem, a short story and an essay every night, for a thousand nights". The idea is to fill your head with ideas and voices, so that you have plenty of inspiration to draw on.

Sometimes, if you're running low on inspiration, it's because you're not reading enough, or trying new experiences. Julia Cameron[46] similarly encourages writers to "fill up the well", as essential nurture for their creativity.

Or, you might try a language challenge. We all have our own language grooves which can sometimes become predictable. Close-reading a new author can introduce fresh flavours, and alert you to new rhythms, styles and vocabulary. Try close-reading favourite authors, too. Often, we're so swept along by great writing and storytelling that we don't spot the techniques in play. Reading as a writer, you'll gain a new appreciation, and new insights for your own writing.

Language used outside your familiar genre – and especially non-fiction – also lends itself to playful mini experiments. Look at the language of recipes, small ads, shopping lists, manuals.

The French experimental writers, *Oulipo*, used creative constraints with language to create new forms and push at the boundaries of human ingenuity. You'll find some examples in **Part 6: Shape & Pattern**.

So there are lots of ways to go with deliberate practice, whatever your writing stage, genre or interests. And you don't need to spend a long time – if five minutes a day is all you have, that's fine.

Think of deliberate practice as a form of play, exercise, meditation or experiment, with a focus on the craft of writing.

Part 3

Doing Deliberate Practice

In this section, you'll find some ways to include deliberate practice in your writing life.

Some are playful, some call for more thought and stretching. Remember, *eustress* is the sweet spot for learning, and **practice** is essential for recall and consolidation. There's more on this in **Part 6: Shape & Pattern**.

By now, you've hopefully got yourself a writer's notebook for your practice, and chosen some topics to start with. If you're unsure, try investigating a couple of thriller writers, and collect a page of energetic verbs. Or collect story openings, ways of describing light, time strategies, intriguing viewpoints.

Decide themes you're drawn to, headline a new page, and start gathering.

Use the front page of each notebook as an index.

Choosing Raw Material

When choosing writing to close-read, you don't have to pick writers who are famous, or best-sellers, or have won literary prizes.

You can do deliberate practice with all kinds of texts and writing genres.

It's best to pick contemporary, professionally published writing you enjoy. Then you'll absorb its energy, and won't be tempted by archaisms, or an overly formal style.

Try historical or technical writing, if you're researching a particular flavour for a specific piece.

Scripts, poetry, magazines, manuals and the backs of cereal packets can give you new ideas for voices and styles to play with. Remember, you're just doing a no-stakes experiment, and it's OK to have fun.

Spoken language forms such as radio and storytelling are great for harvesting character voice rhythms, quirks and individuality. In a similar way, scriptwriters sometimes use "verbatim" techniques to gather authentic characters, voices and material around a theme, before shaping them into a script.[47]

Choose something that inspires or intrigues you, or makes you feel an emotion you're curious about. Make a *deliberate* choice.

Occasionally, I collect poor writing – sometimes from published books. For example, I have a collection of "puppeting" sentences where the author seems to be pulling on the character's strings:

Her eyelids flapped open

A wry smile spread across her face

His head dropped

Looking closer at them, I realised these were all *body part* nouns attached to highly active, gestural verbs – so they conjure clumsy, surreal pictures. The body parts seem to be literally *flapping, spreading* and *dropping*.

Tone down the verb intensity, make the movements smaller, give the verbs less momentum, and the effect isn't so extreme:

Her eyelids flickered open

She gave a wry smile

His head drooped

You may want to pick writers in your genre, to get familiar with tropes and strategies, as inspiration for your own. Or you might want to disrupt the tropes by analysing other writing forms – maybe something contrasting, or counterintuitive.

Language is a living shape-shifter, constantly evolving under our noses.

Be mindful in what you choose – language is infectious!

Picking Your Approach

There are lots of different ways into deliberate practice, as writing has endless dimensions.

Your own practice will be unique to you. Topics I've explored include time, senses, signposting, camera viewpoints, subtext... and authors, including Angela Carter, R.L. Stevenson, Stephen King, and William Shakespeare.

I've mostly used highlighter pens – sometimes buying a second-hand book copy so I don't have hang-ups about defacing it!

More recently, I've built an online app, *Textvizz*, which lets you highlight words easily. See **www.textvizz.com** if you'd like to know more.

If you're writing in a particular genre, you might want to focus on genre-specific techniques – say, pace (*thrillers*), sensuality (*romance*), withholding, plant and payoff (*mystery*).

Or on a general technique – dialogue, description, world-building, characterisation, viewpoint.

Or, choose an author whose work you love, and close-read to discover how they achieve their effects. This can be surprisingly hard to do! You might need to read books twice: once for general enjoyment, and once to focus on technique. Or pick out single paragraphs, and print them out for highlighting.

This kind of close reading is used similarly in film education,[48] as a way to understand elements of a film such as cinematography, editing, narrative structure, and sound.

In the next section, **Patterns and Practice**, you'll find simple examples from my own experiments to try, followed by examples from different scales and dimensions of writing – again, as inspiration for your own experiments.

The technique is extremely versatile, as you'll see, covering everything from word substitution and "cloze"[49] experiments, to emotional impacts, word types, and structural spans.

Patterns and Practice

Here are two suggestions to get you started. They are both kinds of substitution – similar to cloze exercises in language studies.

Example 1: Verb Swap

Find a book sentence where a character is doing something. Then blank out the verbs, and try other verbs in their place.

Here's a sentence by crime author John le Carré:

> *Reaching across the table, Smiley poured two drinks and handed one to Jim.*[50]

Next, highlight or mark up the verbs:

> ***Reaching*** *across the table, Smiley* ***poured*** *two drinks and* ***handed*** *one to Jim.*

This gives you a verb structure to play with:

> *Reaching _____, _____ poured _____ and handed _____.*

There are several things you can try here:

* substitute the verbs with others
* fill in the gaps with different details
* use the language structure to write your own sentences

But first, get a sense of the way the structure feels, by looking closely at the verbs, and what they do.

Read it aloud a few times – the complete sentence, and just the verbs and spaces.

Can you spot the rising action, and then the falling towards the end of the sentence?

What does it feel like if you stop after the comma?

Are you getting a sense of the underlying flow of the sentence?

Next, notice the way the sentence builds a picture of two men (*Smiley and Jim*) in a place (*table*), in relation to each other (*reaching, table, across, to*). So it sets the scene.

What are the parts of speech? Names, nouns, prepositions. More on this later.

Reaching uses the *-ing* form of the verb (*continuous* or *progressive*) to establish an action in progress.

The simple form *-ed* (*poured, handed*) describes one-off, discrete actions.

Combined, the verbs *reaching, poured, handed* create a sense of time sequence (*-ing, -ed, -ed*), with rapid verbs implying a quick, efficient movement. The actions are almost tumbling over each other.

This is economical writing that sets up context in several dimensions at once. It establishes the characters in a quickly sketched visual, with just a few elements, preparing us for the detail to follow.

The transaction between them also creates an effective bridge towards dialogue.

How can you experiment with this powerful sentence structure?

First, brainstorm ten or twenty alternative verbs for each. They don't have to be synonyms – they can be anything you like.

Leaning *across the table*

Stretching
Slobbering
Clambering

Smiley **sloshed** *two drinks*

Downed two drinks
Grabbed
Snatched
Measured
Gulped

> And **handed** one to Jim
>
> *Passed one*
> *Presented*
> *Offered*
> *Thrust*

> **Clambering** *across the table, Smiley* **sloshed** *two*
> *drinks and* **presented** *one to Jim.*

Notice how different verbs change your mental image of the character.

Sloshed suggests careless action and spillage, and evokes the idea of "drunk". *Clambering* evokes physical climbing and the idea of ungainly, clumsy limbs. The verbs manage to suggest that Smiley may be drunk, without actually saying so. A great example of *show*, rather than *tell*!

Do your verb choices make your character seem more or less active? Likeable? Energetic? Capable? What personality traits are suggested by your verbs? What character age and ability? Try different choices, and notice how each choice gives a slightly different picture.

Next, use only the structure ([verb]-*ing*, [verb]-*ed*, and [verb]-*ed*) to create new sentences. For example:

> _____-*ing* , _____-*ed and* _____-*ed*

> **Jumping** *over the sofa, Steve* **grabbed** *two cushions*
> *and* **lobbed** *them at Manon.*

> **Racing** *across the street, Janet* **threw** *two flares and* **set**
> *the sky alight in a blaze of orange.* (irregular verbs)

Note anything you discover. For example, I noticed that the verbs in this structure don't always add up to logic. Janet *racing* across the street while also *throwing flares* and *setting the sky alight* sounds physically challenging, to say the least.

But by piling the actions as though they're almost on top of each other, the writer creates a sense of helter-skelter energy, a blur of chaos. So, the structure is helpful for moving action forward in both time and place.

The cluster of vivid verbs also helps to evoke the main character as a man of action. Smiley gives off a strong sense of purpose and agency.

I noted this example in the "time" page of my notebook. It could equally go under scene-setting, pace or action – whatever you find most helpful.

TRY THIS

Pick a book, author and genre you enjoy, and look for your own examples of time phrases. Scan for sentences that contribute to a sense of time – not just through things and people, but through the structure of language. Analyse the structure, and try cloze and substitution to experiment with your own examples.

Example 2: Time Swap

Choose a long sentence with several clauses. Look out for a sentence with -ing verbs, or time-connective words (*before, after, while, when, until, as soon as*), known as *temporal conjunctions*.

These words point to a time structure. They help to link the other elements of the sentence in time.

Strike out all the words except the time elements.

> *A couple of the younger ones are still munching on their breakfasts, the green juice running down their chins.*[51]

Like this:

> _____ *are still* _____*-ing* _____, _____*-ing* _____.

Now, add your own words into this time pattern. For example:

> *The cars are heading down the road at a stately pace, their black carapaces glinting in the sun.*

> *The birds are still gathering on the wire, squawking loudly.*

Time structures act like a net that can expand to hold other words. They create a kind of scaffold pattern. Analysing and experimenting with patterns is a key method in deliberate practice.

This time pattern feels relatively relaxed, mainly because of the continuous *-ing* verbs, which suggest an ongoing or repeated process, rather than a short, sharp, single action.

Start gathering and practising time structures from the genres you're interested in. Read your sentences aloud, and listen to their music.

Here's a striking, sustained example of *-ing* use from Hilary Mantel's *Wolf Hall*.

> *"She's crying for her idea of what life should be like: Sunday after church, all the sisters, sisters-in-law, wives kissing and patting, swatting at each other's children and at the same time loving them and rubbing their little round heads, women comparing and swapping babies, and all the men gathering and talking business, wool, yarn, lengths, shipping, bloody Flemings, fishing rights, brewing, annual turnover nice timely information, favour-for-favour, little sweeteners, little retainers, my attorney says ..."*[52]

This lovely example evokes a snapshot of timeless actions and traditions which started before the reader arrived, and will continue long after. It's though we've stumbled into a busy, familiar world of reassuring stability. And yet the modal verb *should be* shows that this world is imagined, wishful thinking.

How might you use the *-ing* form of the verb to create a sustained time pattern?

Try adding a modal verb (*might, may, could, should*) to see the effect.

Try past continuous (*was -ing*). Play around with different attributes.

About the author examples

Author examples in this book have been chosen by close reading and highlighting, for the way they illustrate creative and engaging ways of writing, and an underlying language structure for discussion.

These structures are rooted in the syntax and usage of the English language, and aren't unique to those writers. Rather, they are a sense-making shape where writers play their own rhythms, sounds, meanings and stories, just as a musician might use the 12 notes of the Western scale within the 12-bar blues chord structure, to play and create an infinite number of songs.

While this book works with the English language and acknowledges this limitation, the principles can be applied to any language, which each have their own distinct modes and grammars, just as music around the world has microtones, polyrhythms, ragas and many other approaches to tone and structure.

Of course, creative writers don't usually work explicitly with schemata (a notable example being the *Oulipo* avant-garde literary group). But we do use structural and pattern tools, including beat sheets, storylining, the hero's journey, tropes. We use chapters, paragraphs, lines, scenes. We sometimes use rigorous forms such as the sonnet, villanelle, sestina, blank verse, dramatic monologue. We read and view work by other writers, in different media, and absorb structures constantly.

When researching author examples, I was struck by how creatively the writers weave their writing. The structural bones are hidden, practically invisible, below the immersive reader experience. Voice, story, character, atmosphere are foremost. The net disappears, unless you look for it. Yet it holds the creative flow together.

You've already learned writing structures intuitively, by learning language as you grew up. Most people never look deeply into structural patterns. Mostly, we don't need to.

But maybe writers do? This is a time of written language production at an unprecedented scale. First, the explosion of human language on the internet, and now, artificial intelligence.

Maybe it's time for writers to take the lead in revealing the workings of language! Who else is better equipped to show the techniques being used to persuade us, seduce us, change our minds, influence politics, energise or anger us, get into our heads?

Maybe stepping back and getting a look at the tools, the rhetoric, viewpoints, emotions and triggers is essential not just for writers, but also for everyone keen to understand how language is shaping our world? And to show how small word choices can have major resonance and impact?

Whatever your views – maybe you just want to get on with writing your novel! – I feel it's tremendously empowering and refreshing to look at language closely, enjoy its playful ways and expressiveness, music and meanderings, and try something outside your normal grooves.

Part 4

Deliberate Practice Examples

Dimensions of Writing

There are so many dimensions of writing – spatial, interior, exterior, viewpoint, time and temporality, political, social, cultural and economic dimensions, the medium and its technology… and so many more.

It would be impossible to cover them all here, and that's not the point. It's up to you to experiment, discover and adventure.

But to lay foundations for close reading, I'd like to sketch out some territory, beginning with scale.

Scale is particularly important because, as writers, we need to juggle the closeup and distance view at the same time. We're deep in the individual brushstrokes of words, while painting a bigger canvas. A lot of books on writing craft cover larger scale concepts, such as scenes and narrative arcs. Few dig into the scale of words and sentences.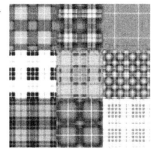

So I'd like to begin with scale, and offer a visual metaphor for the close-up and distance dimensions of writing.

Structure – The Weave of Words

Language is a fascinating weave of elements and ingredients – and the *weaving* metaphor isn't accidental. The words *text* and *textiles* share the same etymology. They're derived from the Latin word *textus͵* meaning "a tissue, web or structure". This in turn comes from *textere*, which means "to weave". So, a text is something woven. And for the practical purposes of this book, a text is woven words.[53]

Interestingly, the "writing as weaving, making" metaphor exists in other cultures, particularly in Indo-European languages.

The Greek word *poesis* means "making". A *poet* is a maker, a creator. In Scotland, poets are sometimes called the old Scots word, *makar*. The Sanskrit word *sutra* means both "thread, string" or "a collection of aphorisms" – strings of word-wisdom.

And in English, writing and textiles have many words in common: *yarn, spin, unravel, cut, thread, twist.*

I find weaving useful for conceptualising the different scales and dimensions of writing. It helps to get a handle (also a textile word!) on how tweaking one element affects the others, just as pulling out a thread, adding a hue, different warp and weft choices fundamentally change the overall impact.

It's interesting to look closely at tweed fabric – made in the region of Scotland I come from – to see how woollen fibres are made from a mix of colours and tiny flecks that give richness and depth. Adding or removing a single colour strand to a woollen yarn changes the look of the entire fabric. Kiltmakers pleat plaid in different ways to foreground different patterns and colours. From a distance, some colours merge, allowing others to emerge more clearly.

This is equally true of other regional patterns made from local palettes of ingredients and tools, whether *Kente* cloth from Ghana or *atlas* fabric from Uzbekistan.

I find this textile metaphor helpful for writing, because it shows different scales and dimensions in play at the same time, and small choices amounting to big impact in the overall picture.

Close reading and deliberate practice will help you to control these impacts more effectively and mindfully.

So, what about scale in writing? Familiar scales we work with include letters, words, phrases, sentences, paragraphs, scenes, and chapters. We also work with *textual elements* such as titles, captions, quotes, and bylines, which help with signposting and structure.

But let's begin with word types, also known as *parts of speech* – nouns, verbs, adjectives, and so on. Don't worry about the terms – they'll be dealt with as they come up.

Each part of speech will give an overview, examples, and some deliberate practice exercises to try. Then we'll move on to larger groupings of words, and finally, some other dimensions, including time and space.

And as we go along, remember the weave of writing: everything is interconnected. Writing space is connected to prepositions. Writing time is connected to verb tenses. You can arrive at the same concept from different angles.

But first, the basic building block: words. And an inspiring quotation from Margaret Atwood:

"A word after a word after a word is power".[54]

Scale – Words

Words can be thought of as primary elements, like musical notes.[55] They can be built together to create phrases and tunes, but – minimalist exceptions aside – they're not the complete work on their own.

Space around individual words makes them stand out. So, they have powerful impact as titles – *Dune* by Frank Herbert; Peter Gabriel's album, *So*; *Frankenstein* by Mary Shelley; *Beloved* by Toni Morrison. They're also impactful as titles for short pieces or segments, such as poems or chapters – *Morning, If, Murder.*

Like a single note, they can ring out, simply be, and leave space for reflection. Without context, they're ambiguous. They haven't resolved towards a particular direction. Their direction of travel isn't clear. This leaves space for the reader to wonder, question, and become engaged.

I find interesting parallels here with artist Paul Klee's concept of the dot and the line in drawing.

In Klee's thinking[56], a dot is a point in space. It's static and lacks direction and dimension. It simply *is*.

A line emerges when a dot begins to move – in Klee's phrase, to "go for a walk". The static dot becomes a dynamic line.

Thinking of language, the word *watch* on its own is open-ended, hanging in space, shimmering with multiple meanings.

watch

Is it a timepiece? A *wrist* timepiece? Or an older one, on a chain? Is it sentry duty? A group of guards? A warning? It's impossible to tell.

But as soon as one word becomes two, it has some context. It has a direction of travel.

> *Watch out, wrist watch, watch chain, night watch,*
> *Black Watch, firewatch.*

For Klee, the dot is pure potential. Even as a static point, it has intrinsic energy. It can be multiplied and grouped, and interact with other elements, such as colour and size.

Similarly, in writing, you might look at the attributes and potential of a single word, and develop them, looking perhaps at number of syllables, hard/soft consonants, vowels, diphthongs, parts of speech, or capitalization.

Or, look at a powerful subgroup of supershort sentences: *imperatives* – verbs used to give commands, instructions, requests, or advice.

> *Duck! Eat. Listen. Go. Wait! Breathe.*

Imperatives are often a single word. Like single-word titles, they carry weight, space and resonance. They can be polite, aggressive, tender, threatening, frustrated, factual.

Imperatives are often monosyllabic, but by no means always.

Exterminate! (the Daleks in Doctor Who)

Geronimo! (inspired by the name of an Apache warrior)

Another powerful subgroup of words that can stand on their own are *interjections.*

Damn! Feck! Fiddlesticks! Yeah! Oh! Yuck!

These are versatile words that express emotions and reactions in a spontaneous way. Like imperatives, they don't have to be a single word or monosyllabic, though they often are.

TRY THIS

Thinking of Klee's dot idea, develop just a single word by looking at its parameters: number of syllables, sounds, types of consonant, vowels, diphthongs, capitalization, spelling... Consider its potentials, meanings and energy. Ask someone else what it evokes for them. How might you disrupt just this single word, without adding another? What changes if the word is only heard, and not seen?

TRY THIS

Watch out for examples of imperatives in your reading or viewing. When might you typically use them yourself? In what sorts of context? Think of *place, status, register, relationship context.* Brainstorm unusual imperatives. Brainstorm three and four-syllable imperatives. Try them with different emotions. Could you use these words in a title or scene? Try the effect of pairing imperatives with gestures – *to reinforce, to subvert, to reject*?

TRY THIS

Write a dialogue exchange using just imperatives. Write a dialogue exchange using single words. In dramatic writing, the technique of short, snappy line exchanges is known as *stichomythia*. When might you use this?

TRY THIS

Think about your characters and how they use imperatives – if they do. Do the characters wind people up? How are they respected? If they don't use imperatives, why not? What might they use instead, for the language functions of *command, instruct, request, advise*? What circumstances would drive them to use imperatives? Try the effect of imperatives to open or end a scene.

TRY THIS

Experiment with other kinds of single-word expressions – expletives (*damn, shit*), adjectives (*gross, beautiful*), names, numbers, interjections (*woo! eh? phew!*), interrogatives (*when? what? how?*). Try the effect of short and long words. What would your character typically use? What would be untypical or disruptive? Try the effect at the start or end of a scene. Try sonic effects – plosive sounds (*k, d, t, g*), fricatives (*wh, sh, th, ff*), voiced/unvoiced (*v/ff, g/k*). Try them in people's names and place names.

Scale – Phrases

At the next language scale, let's look at phrases – small groups or "chunks" of words that make up a sense unit.

Everyday examples include:

> *How are you doing?*
> *Last night...*
> *Go straight ahead.*
> *Just a minute.*

More complex phrases from earlier in this book include:

> *what life should be like*
> *still munching on their breakfasts*
> *ever-evolving neurons*
> *how it might be applied to writing*

Breaking language into phrases or chunks isn't an exact science. You'll have your own rhythm and sense of how words group together for you.

What's more important is that these phrase-chunks *have* rhythm. They're a bit like musical phrases, or fragments of song, with tiny moments of space between. And we use them constantly.

Research has shown that language chunking, or semantic chunking (that is, into *meaning* groups), helps with language learning, by reducing cognitive load[57]. Chunks also play an important part in language recall and retention.

This contemporary thinking is a significant break from the older language learning approaches based on isolated words in dictionaries, and grammar rules, which many of us have encountered.

More recent thinking suggests that although we do learn individual words, we don't painstakingly piece them together through an understanding of grammar. We learn chunks and sequences – short bursts of words that often occur together. Gradually, we extend our range, group larger chunks together, introduce less frequent words into our learned patterns. And if we practice the language enough, we become fluent – *flowing*.

To explain how much easier this is than learning individual vocabulary, here's an example from when I learned German at school.

We were learning the phrase *by train*, which in German is "mit dem Zug" – *with the train*. For a beginner, the grammar of this simple phrase is *hard*. We had to learn – and prepare to glaze over – that *train* is a masculine word, and that *with* takes the dative case (whatever that is), which changes *der* to *dem*. So, you get "mit dem Zug".

By the time you've worked out how to say "by train" using grammar, the train has long ago left the station.

But if you listen to what people actually *say*, you'll hear the words *mit dem Zug* all the time. Did you travel *mit dem Zug*? How did you get here? *Mit dem Zug.*

So it's far quicker to just learn the phrase and ignore the grammar. Then you can try swapping in other words: *mit dem*

Taxi, mit dem Bus, mit dem Auto... Wow! It works! Then one day, you hear *mit der U-Bahn* – what's that? *The underground*. Not *mit dem U-Bahn*? No – *mit der U-Bahn*. Then you might go to your grammar, and grapple with feminine noun and the dative case (whatever that is). But in the meantime, you've caught your train.

That's just an example to show that patterns and chunks are a faster, more effective way to learn. This doesn't just apply to second language learning. It applies equally to a deliberate practice approach to writing.

What do writing and speaking feel like to you? For me, "phrases and chunks" feels about right. Hesitations, then bursts of words. Pauses, then rushes. Maybe if I were a super-experienced public speaker, I'd be able to control this jumpy rhythm and speak in a measured, well-paced way. But I'd still feel the jumpy, "saccade" thought process happening underneath.

Writing feels similar, to me: pauses for thought, then bursts.

Touch-typing feels physically much like playing a musical instrument. Some words – *the, and, we, go* – feel like small flutters that don't need any thought. In that respect, the activity of writing is similar to anything you do frequently – driving a car, making coffee, having a shower in the morning. Writing is made up of chunks of the familiar, and pauses for the less familiar.

So, from a deliberate practice viewpoint, chunks and phrases are powerful language segments for fast-tracking your learning.

Let's look now at some examples of different kinds of phrases. Bear in mind that these are my highly individual real usage examples, chosen to illustrate patterns. They are descriptive, not prescriptive. I hope you'll go on to find your own examples and categories.

Phrase-based thinking may be helpful if you're researching characters who use terminology you're unfamiliar with. Say you're writing someone who keeps bees, mends clocks… look out for chunks of language, as well as individual words. Gathering language with its immediate context will include its rhythms, and possibly a sense of viewpoint, helping your writing to feel more authentic. Theatre writers sometimes gather "verbatim" material for scripts in this way.[58]

Now for a look at some *types* of phrase, from a language point of view.

Personal Phrases and Catchphrases

These are short, usually informal expressions that become part of a person's signature style.

> *What's up?*
> *Take care!*
> *Hang in there.*
> *It's all good.*
> *My bad.*

As you can see, they're often used to express emotions and attitudes. Some personal phrases are so memorable that they become catchphrases, indelibly linked to a character, and sometimes even stand as a shorthand reference to a film or story.

> *I'll be back.*[59]
> *Curiouser and curiouser!*[60]
> *Here's Johnny!*[61]
> *You had me at hello.*[62]
> *Bite me!*[63]

Some phrases are so vivid and memorable that they enter everyday language, and their origins fade over time. *Break the ice, in a pickle, to wear your heart on your sleeve, good riddance, too much of a good thing…* - they're all phrases found in Shakespeare's plays, yet are widely used today.

Sometimes, catchphrases are used in a self-aware or ironic way. The person speaking *knows* they're repeating a catchphrase, and possibly a cliché. One of my friends in Germany once said, "Good thinking, Batman!" I'd never heard the phrase before, and the memory of him using it has stayed with me. He's a science fiction fan, so I assumed it came from the films, or the 1960s TV series. But researching this book, I discovered that it was never a catchphrase on the show. It's more of an affectionate parody phrase inspired by the playful banter between Batman and Robin.

Catchphrases can be taken even further, to an ironic extreme – an effect often used in comedy, sometimes in a meta-humorous or absurdist way. For example, the British comedy series, *The Fast Show*, is well known for playing with comedy conventions by creating new, plausible-sounding catchphrases that don't necessarily make sense. You may find these catchphrases from comedy and entertainment shows familiar:

> *Computer says no.*[64]
> *I'll get me coat.*[65]
> *How you doin'?*[66]
> *Sashay away.*[67]

TRY THIS

Listen out for characteristic phrases that people use, and note them down. Brainstorm different ways of saying the same thing – except, of course, it's never exactly the same! Dig into what's distinctive about this choice. What does it suggest about the speaker's character? What mental map, metaphor or influence does it suggest? What happens if you change one of the words in the phrase?

TRY THIS

Explore the cliché qualities of phrases and catchphrases you find. Is the catchphrase used ironically or with self-awareness? Affectionately, or sarcastically? Brainstorm different ways it can be spoken, with different emotions, by different characters.

TRY THIS

Choose a phrase and explore repetition and transformation, to give it a "journey" over time. For example, in the movie Casablanca[68], the main character, Rick Blaine, says "Here's looking at you, kid" several times, with its context changing each time. It takes on the quality of a refrain in a song or poem, resonating differently and growing complex layers, as it chimes with different moments in the film. How might you use this technique? What happens if you give a phrase to a different character?

Functional Phrases

Functional phrases are everyday expressions used in basic communication. They're usually short and have a clear purpose.

> *Excuse me.*
> *How much is it?*
> *I don't understand.*
> *Could you help me?*
> *What time is it?*

Since these are everyday phrases, they don't typically stand out. But you can also exploit this very quality, in different ways – perhaps by using them in a situation where they're unusual, comedic or transgressive.

Consider, for example, someone who struggles with communication, and is suddenly able to speak a usually banal phrase. This happens near the end of the film *The King's Speech*. King George VI, who has a severe stutter, delivers a wartime speech to the nation, then turns to his speech therapist and says, "Thank you."

In the film *Lost in Translation*[69], Charlotte is trying to navigate everyday interactions while living in Japan as someone who can't speak the language. Her broken use of simple phrases reinforces her isolation and difficulty in connecting.

In *Thor: Ragnarok*[70], Thor is known for incongruously using everyday phrases that show the mismatch between his Asgard culture and contemporary life on Earth. When he wants another coffee, he shouts "Another!" and smashes his coffee mug to the ground. He uses learned politeness in incongruous settings: "Do you have a phone I could use?" or "do you have Wi-Fi?" have great comedic effect if they're used by a Norse god who travels through different dimensions.

Other examples of everyday phrases transformed include "Hello, Clarice", from *The Silence of the Lambs*[71], "Run!" from *Forrest Gump*[72], and the repeated "It's not your fault" from *Good Will Hunting*.[73]

Subverting familiar language is another way to explore and invent phrases. Online culture is full of examples, like the meme "I can has cheezburger?", which, if you're not active on social media, might sound nonsensical. Let's just say it's a speaking cat!

TRY THIS

Find examples from books or films where ordinary phrases are changed by the context. Consider the emotional impact – pathos, bathos, comedy, surrealism, connection? Now choose a phrase or catchphrase you use a lot. Brainstorm some scene ideas where you could transform its impact. Who might speak it? What kind of character are they? Are they normally communicative, or do they struggle?

TRY THIS

Most functional phrases have a goal in mind, whether to get a coffee, focus the attention, exchange politeness, establish status... Choose a phrase, and decide its typical goal. Brainstorm scenarios where the phrase doesn't work as expected. Why not? What expectations do the characters bring to the exchange? What kind of characters are they?

TRY THIS

Functional phrases aren't always used between people. Sometimes, people (including you!) use these phrases on their own, speaking to themselves, or to someone who isn't there, or can't reply. Choose a phrase you might overhear someone using, or might use when you're on your own. Brainstorm scenarios where this ordinary phrase might stand out – try using contrast, incongruity, disruption of expectation, different context... What happens next? Write this scene.

Scale and beyond

Single words, short phrases and chunking are at one end of the scale of language. See what you can discover from looking at this small, closeup scale of language.

Then, you'll want to look at what connects the chunks together – connectors such as *conjunctions* and *relative pronouns*.

This moves us on to the scale of *sentences* and *paragraphs* – sustained flows of language that can be combined in infinite possible expressive and creative ways.

But as well as scale, it's good to dive into different *types* of words – word classes, categories, or parts of speech – and what they can do.

Nouns, verbs, adjectives, conjunctions – all have very different functions. The next section gives you an overview of the main parts of speech used in *Textvizz*, and some experiments to try.

Conjunctions (*and, but, or, so, because, although*) are included in **Part 5**, under **Word Classes**. Relative pronouns (*which, who, that, whose*) are such an expansive topic for creating sustained writing flow that they're covered in **Part 6** under **Net Bags**.

Part 5

Language Topics

Word Classes (Parts of Speech)

Words can be divided into different categories, often called "parts of speech". If you've ever learned grammar, you'll be familiar with *verbs, nouns, adjectives, adverbs…* and there are a good few more. It can get pretty arcane and detailed, and you might even be a bit apprehensive about these terms, especially if they remind you of school.

Rest assured – you're not alone, and I won't go there! I've met a lot of writers who feel that way about grammar. I've only gone into it myself because I learned other languages and taught English as a foreign language, so I had to learn its grammar.

And once I did, as a writer, I found it fascinating. Who knew that all these amazing shapes, tones and structures are going on under the surface?

I've noticed that in the last decade or so, there's been a revival of grammar teaching in secondary education. Studies have shown that knowing more about the basics of language as a *system* can help people to write and communicate more easily and effectively. And teaching styles have also moved on, just as they have in maths and other subjects.

The first time I heard a secondary student say their favourite subject was maths, I was amazed! How on earth could you possibly love maths?! But looking at the new methods, interactive teaching, gamification, online bitesize tutorials – it all looks much more fun.

And I'd like to think this is happening with language, too.

First, a super-quick reminder about terminology used in this section. It's a really helpful shorthand for studying language and style.

The following main word classes, or *parts of speech*, are used in my *Textvizz* app – see **www.textvizz.com**.

Nouns

A noun is a naming word – whether of people, places, things, or ideas. It's easy to remember, as *noun* and **name** are pretty well the same word. They come from the same root: *nama* in old English.

Examples: *cat, city, love.*

If you want to go deeper, here are the main different kinds of nouns:

- *concrete* nouns (*cat, city, music*) – things you can feel with your senses
- *abstract* nouns (*love, freedom, happiness*) – concepts and qualities
- *countable* nouns (*apple/apples, car/cars, person/people*) – things that can be counted, and have both singular and plural forms
- *mass* or *uncountable* nouns (*water, air, information*) – things that can't be counted individually
- *collective* nouns (*team, flock, family, bunch*) – a collection of people, animals or things considered as a unit
- *proper* nouns (*Kentucky, Edinburgh, the BBC, the Eiffel Tower*) – specific names of people, places, organisations or things. These typically have capital letters.

Verbs

Verbs are *action* or *being* words. Again, this is easy to remember by thinking of *verb* and *verve*. Verbs are spirited, alive, in motion – even if you *sit, read, be, see,* or *feel*, you're doing something active. Even if the verb is in the past tense, it's still an action.

Examples: *run, crash, sit, ran, crashed, sat, am writing, was eating.*

Nouns and verbs are especially weighty words, as they carry the bulk of meaning in a sentence – the information about *who* and *what's happening.* The actions, and who or what is doing them.

The next-weightiest word class, in my opinion (and as you'll see, I'm not alone): *prepositions.*

Prepositions

Prepositions are words such as *in, under, with, at.* Although they're tiny, everyday words, they punch above their weight in terms of meaning, because they explain how things *relate* to each other.

Some more examples: *on, at, beyond, before, from… to, with, despite, due to.*

Prepositions connect things in *space, time* or *logic.*

If you imagine noun-things as beads on a net, and verbs as the action-threads between, prepositions are the knots that connect the threads together.

So, with just those three parts of speech – nouns, verbs, prepositions – you've already set up crucial cornerstones of meaning: who-what, what they're doing, and their interconnection.

The idea of words as a net with notes and connectors may be familiar. You'll see similar analogies used for brain activity, the internet, and the structure of molecules.

When I investigated visuals to represent the many dimensions of language, I had a Eureka moment: the Semantic Web!

The *Semantic Web*[74] – the web of *meaning* – was invented to help search engines to give better, more meaningful results. Instead of just doing a keyword match, it interprets the relationships between things.

In the early days of the internet, search engines were very hit-or-miss. You put in the word or phrase, fingers crossed – you get a match for those words. But not necessarily those meanings – the words *lead* as in "leader" and *lead* as in "lead piping" looked exactly the same to search engines.

The Semantic Web is different. And – fascinating for writers – it uses a search approach based on language categories. In very simplified terms, it's looking for *entities* (represented by *nouns*) and *relationships* between them (*actions* and *connections*, similar to *verbs* and *prepositions*).

Nouns, verbs, prepositions! I was mind-blown to see my instinct confirmed: certain word classes have extra-powerful semantic weight. And this thinking is in everyday use on the internet.

After this weighty group of *nouns, verbs, prepositions*, let's look at two categories about *describing*: *adjectives* and *adverbs*. Think of them as words that *add* something to other words.[75]

Adjectives

Adjectives are used to describe or modify nouns.

Examples: *happy* cat, *blue* planet, *devastating* news.

Adverbs

Adverbs are used to modify verbs or adjectives. Again, think of them as *adding* something. Adverbs often end in -*ly* – *quickly, slowly*. Many common adverbs don't, though – *always, here, outside*.[76]

Examples: *quickly* running, *clumsily* reaching for the glasses, *quite* beautiful, *so* annoying.

Articles

Articles are extremely common words in English: *the, a* and *an*. That's it![77]

It's easier to grasp what they do by imagining languages without them – for example, Russian.

You might hear a Russian native speaker say "I saw dog in park yesterday" or "I bought television in supermarket". Why? Because Russian doesn't have the English articles: *the, a, an*.

So, what do these tiny words do? They're determiners. They *determine* whether the noun is *specific*, or *unspecific*.

For example:

> *I saw **the** dog yesterday*

Compared with

> *I saw **a** dog yesterday*

*I saw **the** dog* conjures a specific dog – maybe your own dog, or a neighbour's. You want to refer to just that dog, as in:

> *I saw that-there dog.*

*I saw **a** dog* refers to a dog in general.

> *I saw a random dog.*

An works the same as *a*, except it's used for nouns starting with vowels (*a, e, i, o, u*). The *n* evolved over time, because it's hard to say *a apple, a ink bottle.*

> *I saw an adorable dog.*

> *An orange, an actor, an unidentified object.*

Of course, if you're a native speaker of English, this is intuitive for you. Everyone else has to learn it. But being mindful of your choice between the tiny words *a* and *the* can make a big difference to your meaning.

Up ahead, we'll look at some examples and ways to play with articles through deliberate practice.

Conjunctions

Conjunctions are connectors – as the name suggests, they *conjoin* other words or phrases.

Examples: *and, but, or.*

> *I could go to the movies tonight, **or** I could stay at home and tidy the house.*

There are three main kinds. Here's a quick overview – or skip it, and note it as a reference for later:

Coordinating conjunctions are used to link sentences or clauses of equal importance:

> *for, and, nor, but, or, yet, so.*

> *I like tea **and** coffee. I went to the supermarket **but** it was raining.*

People sometimes use the mnemonic FANBOYS to remember these: *for, and, nor, but, or, yet, so.*

Subordinating conjunctions are used when one clause is dependent on, or subordinate to, another.

> *Because, although, since, when, if, while.*

> *I didn't go to the supermarket, **because** it was raining.*

The ideas are causally linked. Compare:

> *I went to the supermarket **but** it was raining.*

The two phrases are independent. It feels like:

> *I went to the supermarket **but** – as it randomly happens – it was raining.*

Correlative conjunctions come in balanced pairs.

Examples: *either/or, neither/nor, both/and, not only/but also.* Don't worry about this detail – return later on, when you've gathered some examples.

And here's one final everyday word class:

Interjections

Oh! Wow! Ouch! Interjections express emotion or exclamation. Think of them as tiny *inter*ruptions. They often stand alone, or at the beginning of a sentence.

That's it! A refresher on the main parts of speech.

This topic can get very detailed and granular, if you want to go there. And words don't always fit into simple categories, with linguists often debating whether to put words in one category or another.[78] Meanings can overlap; words and meanings can shapeshift as fast as words are produced.[79]

That's all the more reason to be playful with words, and take your cue from how they're used around you, and your own creative instincts.

Parts of speech are a useful tool that can help you to see, create and disrupt patterns.

TRY THIS

Choose one of the parts of speech in this section. Now, choose a few sentences from a writer you're interested in. Check back to the *Verb Swap* and *Time Swap* examples in **Part 2**. Now, try the same technique, using your own examples. For example, if you're interested in how a writer connects phrases and chunks together – the *glue* of writing, as it were – create *cloze* or gap patterns with only the conjunctions or relative pronouns visible. Collect examples from different writers and see how they achieve flow. Create your own sentences by adapting the patterns you find. Which are close to your own flow and rhythm? Which would you never use? What can you learn about your own voice and style? Modals (*can, could, will, should, must*) are another interesting part of speech to look closely at, as they can reveal a mood of possibility, certainty or obligation.

Time Flow

Time flow patterns are some of the most powerful structures in writing. They help to situate the action in time, creating a clear timeline for the reader. They can also handle momentary flashback and flashforward, and drive action on, giving a sense of momentum to keep the reader engaged.

Here are some patterns to try.

Time Pattern 1

> *First, he completed the research; then, he compiled the data into a report.*

> *First, _____ -ed _____; then, _____ -ed_____.*

Now, try the future:

> *First, _____ will _____; then, _____ will _____.*

Now try *modal* – the *"if"*, speculative, conditional mood:

> *First, _____ would (should, might) _____then, _____ would _____.*

Time Pattern 2 - Sequence of Actions 2

> *In the morning, she attended meetings, and in the afternoon, she worked on her projects.*

> *In the morning, _____-ed _____, and in the afternoon, _____-ed _____.*

> *In the morning, _____ will _____, and in the afternoon, _____ will _____.*

> *In the morning, _____ could (would, should, might) _____, and in the afternoon, _____ will _____.*

Now, swap out the time phrases:

> *Yesterday, _____-ed _____, and at four o'clock, _____-ed _____*

> *To begin with, _____-ed; next, _____-ed.*

Author examples

"...in the morning THE WHOLE KIPPS FAMILY have breakfast together and a conversation TOGETHER and then get into a car TOGETHER (are you taking notes?)"
  Zadie Smith, "On Beauty"

"During our first winter I hired a family instead of a single man."
  Stephen King, "The Shining"

"This was the first morning of summer."
  Ray Bradbury, "Dandelion Wine"

"One night each week he was allowed to leave his father, his mother, and his younger brother Tom asleep in their small house next door and run here, up the dark spiral stairs to his grandparents' cupola."
  Ray Bradbury, "Dandelion Wine"

"...to climb the Radley front steps and call, 'He-y', of a Sunday afternoon was something their neighbours never did."
  Harper Lee, "To Kill a Mockingbird"

"In those early amorphous years when memory had only just begun, when life was full of Beginnings and no Ends, and Everything was For Ever, Esthappen and Rahel thought of themselves together as Me, and separately, individually, as We or Us."
  Arundhati Roy, "The God of Small Things"

Simultaneous actions

While cooking dinner, she listened to a podcast.

While _____ -ing _____, _____ -ed _____.

As the sun set, they gathered around the campfire, sharing stories.

As _____, _____-ed _____.

Now that the sun had set, the city lights began to illuminate the skyline.

Now that _____ had _____, _____ began _____.

Now that _____ was _____, _____.

During the meeting, he took notes to capture key points.

During _____, _____.

With the garden completely cleared of ground elder, it was time to plant the potatoes.

With _____, it was time to _____.

With _____, _____ could _____.

Author examples

"With buckets half burdened with fox grapes and wild strawberries, followed by bees which were, no more, no less, said Father, the world humming under its breath, they sat on a green-mossed log..."
  Ray Bradbury, "Dandelion Wine"

"While crossing one particularly unkind box, I heard around me the cries of an animal in pain..."
  Kazuo Ishiguro, "Klara and the Sun"

"During the several years he had spent in British jails during the struggle for Independence..."
  Vikram Seth, "A Suitable Boy"

Foregrounding in the present

Sometimes you might want to draw a line under the past, and pull strong focus on the present moment – perhaps for description, or capturing the current state of play. Here's a useful technique:

Now _____

Everything was ready – equipment, provisions, dogs fed and watered. Now it was time to start.

Now here was the very person they'd been waiting for.

Now we had our team lined up. If you could call Jac, Freya and Dan a team.

Author example

"Now here was this woman with the presence of mind to repair a dog gone savage with pain rocking her crossed ankles and looking away from her own daughter's body."
Toni Morrison, "Tonight"

Time Conjunctions (Joining Words)

By next week, she will have finished the first draft of her latest novel.

By _____, _____ will have _____ -ed _____

By _____, _____ will _____

After _____, _____ -ed.

When _____, _____ was _____

As _____, _____ -ed

Author examples

"Dearest Anne, by the time you get this I will be married."
Shirley Jackson, "The Daemon Lover"

"After a wait long enough for someone to get out of a comfortable chair, a woman joined him in the doorway, regarding the dark hall."
Shirley Jackson, "The Daemon Lover"

> *"She was halfway down the first flight of stairs when the door was opened and Mrs Royster shouted down the stairwell."*
> Shirley Jackson, *"The Daemon Lover"*

> *"Edgar went to the phone to call someone. Then he said, 'Open her purse, see if you can find where she's staying.'"*
> Raymond Carver, *"Put Yourself in My Shoes"*

> *"Just as I entered, the new peer, appearing silently out of nowhere, approached this daunting figure."*
> Jan Morris, *"A Writer's World"*

> *"As our journey proceeded, though, I began to doubt if the Neapolitans were beaten after all."*
> Jan Morris, *"A Writer's World"*

Participial Phrases

-ing and *-ed* clauses can be used at the start of a sentence to give more information about the subject of the sentence – say, one of your characters. They suggest the subject is doing two things at once, and create a sense of anticipation.

Careful! Although this structure looks straightforward, it's often used wrongly. See the note on "dangling modifiers" at the end of this section.

> *Walking briskly, he reached the bus station just in time.*

> *Reading the novel, he discovered quite a few typos that he wished had been put right before publication.*

> _____ -ing _____, _____ -ed _____.

> *Excited by the news, she called her bestie Sarah right away.*

> *Terrified at the thought, he stowed the camcorder in a locked storage box and hid it under the bed.*

> _____ -ed _____, _____ -ed _____.

112

Author examples

"He at once checked the horses and, jumping to the ground, disappeared into the darkness."
    Bram Stoker, "Dracula"

"While crossing one particularly unkind box, I heard around me the cries of an animal in pain…"
    Kazuo Ishiguro, "Klara and the Sun"

Caution! Dangling Modifiers!

With participial phrases, one subject is actioning both verbs. A "dangling modifier" happens when two different subjects are actioning the verbs. For example:

"Hanging the painting on the wall, the squeaky nail caused a disturbance in the room."

Here, it sounds as though the squeaky nail is hanging the painting. This doesn't make sense. This next example is correct:

"Hanging the painting on the wall, Fred admired his handiwork."

Fred, the subject of the sentence, is doing both: "hanging" and "admiring".

Test Yourself: Spot the Dangling Modifier

1a. Haring down the street, she saw the last bus pull out of the station.

b. Haring down the street, the last bus pulled out of the station.

2a. Being late for the meeting, the car wouldn't start.

b. Being late for the meeting, I found that the car wouldn't start.

3a. Confused by the complicated instructions, the recipe turned out all wrong.

b. Confused by the instructions, he found that the recipe turned out all wrong.

Answers: 1a, 2b and 3b are correct. 1b, 2a and 3a are examples of dangling modifiers.

Using "With"

With every whispered conversation, Maria gained more and more snippets of information about the mysterious world beyond the walls of the overgrown garden.

With every new milestone, Carter felt more confident.

With _____, _____ -ed _____.

With _____, _____ became (becomes) _____.

Author examples

"Meg got behind his chair under pretense of smoothing the wrinkles out of his tired forehead, and standing there, she said, with her panic increasing with every word..."
   Louisa M. Alcott, "Little Women"

"With buckets half burdened with fox grapes and wild strawberries, followed by bees which were, no more, no less, said Father, the world humming under its breath, they sat on a green-mossed log..."
   Ray Bradbury, "Dandelion Wine"

"Within two months, in the dead of winter, leaving their grandmother, Baby Suggs; Sethe, their mother; and their little sister Denver, all by themselves in the gray and white house on Bluestone Road."
   Toni Morrison, "Tonight"

"With that, in a manner of speaking the introduction was made."
   John le Carré, "Tinker Tailor Soldier Spy"

*"With less than a blink, his face seemed to change -
underneath it lay the activity."*
  Toni Morrison, "Tonight"

Cause and Effect

This cause-effect pattern also gives a sense of events happening at
around the same time.

> *Because it was raining heavily, the event was
> postponed.*
>
> *Because they couldn't all fit in the small car, some of the
> volunteers decided to walk.*
>
> *Because _____, _____ -ed _____.*
>
> *Due to the traffic jam, she arrived late for the meeting.*
>
> *Due to circumstances beyond our control, we've decided
> that there's no option but to withdraw the team from
> the competition.*
>
> *Due to _____, _____ -ed _____.*

Author example

> *"Because it's such a small set-up, I get to work closely with
> him."*
>   *Zadie Smith, "On Beauty"*

Inverted Word Order

> *Never before had they witnessed such a spectacular
> performance.*
>
> *Never before had _____. Only after hours of searching
> did they find the missing keys.*
>
> *Only after _____ did _____.*

115

Author example

> *"It was only in the exact bottom of the dell and round the tavern door that a thin veil still hung unbroken."*
> *R.L. Stevenson, "Treasure Island"*

Repeated Actions

This pattern is used to describe regular habits. The use of *would*, instead of the simple past tense, creates a slight air of melancholy. The habit seems fuzzy, as though seen through distant fond memory, compared with the direct, factual mood of *they took, she baked.*

> *Every weekend, they would take long walks in the park.*

> *Every weekend, they took long walks in the park.*

> *Every _____, they (she, he, it) would _____.*

> *On her birthday, she would bake a chocolate cake from scratch.*

> *On _____ days, she (they, he) would _____.*

> *Each week, they would put fresh jars of jam into the cupboard. By the end of the summer, it was full.*

> *Each _____, they'd _____.*

> *Every _____, she'd always _____.*

Author examples

> *"Madame Ratignolle had been married seven years. About every two years she had a baby."*
> *Kate Chopin, "The Awakening"*

> *"…every now and again he drummed up a pretext to bring him to the city."*
> *Kate Chopin, "The Awakening"*

> *"Every few moments I could hear the yelpings of the dogs."*
> *Northrup Solomon, "12 Years A Slave"*

"He carried his own low temperature always about with him."

    Charles Dickens, "A Christmas Carol"

"The telephone lines between here and Sidewinder are still above ground and they go down almost every winter at some point or other and are apt to stay down for three weeks to a month and a half."

    Stephen King, "The Shining"

"Two hours later Lansquenet-sous-Tannes is invisible once more, like an enchanted village which appears only once every year."

    Joanne Harris, "Chocolat"

Each man he asks stares at his face, steps back and says, 'You tell me!'

    Hilary Mantel, "Wolf Hall"

Flashback/flashforward

With skilful verb use, you can zip around in time, and establish the narrator's vantage point. Maybe they're looking back on the story events from a great distance:

When I turned 18, I cut off my long, dark hair and dumped it in a wheelie bin.

When _____, _____ and _____-ed _____.

In the future, we'll all have memory implants and regular brain upgrades.

In the future, _____ will _____.

By the time we're 60, we expect to have our own house and our first grandchild.

By the time he reached the café, she had already left.

By the time _____, _____.

117

Author examples:

"When they saw him coming on, (they) would tug their owners into doorways and up courts..."
  Charles Dickens, "A Christmas Carol"

"...when I tried to move towards it, I realized it was in fact two cones, one inserted into the other."
  Kazuo Ishiguro, "Klara and the Sun"

"When the last of the chamomile was gone, she went around to the front of the house, collecting her shoes and stockings on the way."
  Toni Morrison, "Tonight"

"When she laughed it came out loose and young."
  Toni Morrison, "Tonight"

"By the time he reached his study however, Thursgood's laughter had quite worn off and he became extremely nervous."
  John le Carré, "Tinker Tailor Soldier Spy"

"They went by Mongibello last year when they were on a cruise. Richard promised he'd come home when the winter began."
  Patricia Highsmith, "The Talented Mr Ripley"

"In the following weeks, the weeks when he examined every corner of the bungalow, when he discovered that a beehive was lodged in the cashew tree..."
  Chimamanda Ngozi Adichie, "Half of a Yellow Sun"

"...as Jim wrestled with an off-side prop in the course of that same summer term, the boys paid Jim the compliment of a nickname..."
  Chimamanda Ngozi Adichie, "Half of a Yellow Sun"

Spatial Flow

Spatial flow is the second key dimension needed to anchor the reader in your world. Anchoring your reader in time and space will go a long way towards allowing them to see your world clearly.

Readers need secure anchors, so that they can confidently follow your writing. Otherwise, they'll get confused, and simply give up on your book.

All genres need some kind of anchoring – even fantasy and speculative fiction, where writers make the rules and build the world from scratch.

Even unreliable narrators, shifting reality and experimental fiction need some degree of anchoring – some kind of structure to lead the reader through what would otherwise be chaos.

Here's the famous opening of George Orwell's dystopian novel, *1984*.

> *"It was a bright cold day in April and the clocks were striking thirteen."*

Right away, Orwell signposts that we're not in an ordinary world. With brilliant economy, he sketches in a context for his reader to imagine. The strange image primes us for further strange things to happen.

He also sets the stage for his main character, Winston Smith, to appear.

Without context, a character is floating in a vacuum. The reader, too, is unmoored and uncertain. This is fine for a very short while. But if this continues, the reader can't see the pictures you're building. They need a thread to follow through what would otherwise be chaos. We need a sense of their surroundings.

Even a single word helps to create a picture for the reader.

Shakespeare's stage directions are a good example of economical scene-setting.

> *A blasted heath.*

You don't necessarily need full description of a place to establish basic spatial anchoring. Detail can come later.

Here are some evocative examples from novels.

> "We came on the wind of the carnival."
> Joanne Harris, "Chocolat"

> "It was a quiet morning, the town covered over with darkness and at ease in bed."
> Ray Bradbury, "Dandelion Wine"

> "Tom glanced behind him and saw the man coming out of the Green Cage, heading his way."
> Patricia Highsmith, "The Talented Mr Ripley"

> "'So now get up.'" Felled, dazed, silent, he has fallen; knocked full length on the cobbles of the yard."
> Hilary Mantel, "Wolf Hall"

> "May in Ayemenem is a hot, brooding month. The days are long and humid. The river shrinks and black crows gorge on bright mangoes in still, dustgreen trees."
> Arundhati Roy, "The God of Small Things"

> "'You too will marry a boy I choose,' said Mrs Rupa Mehra firmly to her younger daughter. Lata avoided the maternal imperative by looking around the great lamp-lit garden of Prem Nivas. The wedding guests were gathered on the lawn."
> Vikram Seth, "A Suitable Boy"

> "The truth is, if old Major Dover hadn't dropped dead at Taunton races Jim would never have come to Thursgood's at all."
> John le Carré, "Tinker Tailor Soldier Spy"

What do you notice? I notice place-names, of course, but let's dig deeper. The place-names in these examples are mostly unfamiliar to me, and evoke a language and culture. They're not just signposts for specific places, but also descriptive, colourful and musical.

Place-names will resonate very differently for different readers. If you're familiar with the place, the name will act as a lightning rod for memories or cultural knowledge. If you're not familiar with the place, its name's musical qualities may evoke a picture, or other sensory impression.

But readers still need spatial orientation. Notice that each example also has general place nouns: *carnival, town, yard, river/trees, garden/lawn, races.*

These "broadbrush" words help to set the context. They're broad enough to anchor new knowledge in something familiar to readers – a known context – to make it easy to understand and remember.

This might sound abstract. But practically, how are you setting context for readers so far unfamiliar with your world? You don't need to give away everything about the place you're creating. But signalling the *kind of place* will really help your reader get "cogged" with your story. This is especially important if you're writing about less familiar worlds in history, geography, fantasy or science fiction.

Author examples

"When he woke in the woods in the dark and the cold of the night he'd reach out to touch the child sleeping beside him."
    Cormac McCarthy, *"The Road"*

"'No! I don't want the mangosteen,'" Anderson Lake leans forward, pointing. 'I want that one, there. Kaw pollamai nee khap. The one with the red skin and the green hairs.'"
    Paolo Bacigalupi, *"The Windup Girl"*

"The body lay naked and facedown, a deathly gray, spatters of blood staining the snow around it."
    Ann Leckie, *"Ancillary Justice"*

"The Red Union had been attacking the headquarters of the April Twenty-eight Brigade for two days." -
    Cixin Liu, *"The Three-Body Problem"*

"The King stood in a pool of blue light, unmoored."
    Emily St John Mandel, *"Station Eleven"*

Titles, too, can help powerfully with spatial orientation. Place-names are wonderfully evocative, but how about general place words?

> **Dune** – *immediately evokes a sand world.*

> **The Priory of the Orange Tree** – *we're in a religious order.*

> **The Lion, the Witch and the Wardrobe** – *a familiar space that turns out to be a magical gateway.*

Or, try evoking place through people or things that have strong associations with it.

> **A Game of Thrones** – *thrones! We're in a royal court.*

> **Parable of the Sower** – *a field of grain.*

> **The Prisoner of Azkaban** – *a jail.*

TRY THIS

Write some book and chapter titles using place-names, as well as general and specific place words. What images do they evoke? Read them aloud to feel their sonic qualities. Try them out on someone else and ask what images they evoke. What genre is suggested? What kind of characters? What potential readership? Are the mood, genre and readers aligned to your intentions for your book?

Prepositions – Space Connectors

If you want to build clearer spatial connections and anchors in your writing, look at prepositions of place – words such as *in, on, through, into, by, with, under,* etc.

Prepositions are a category of words used to show a relationship in space, time or logic, between people, places, or things.

> *The cat sat on the mat.*

He went into the woods.

They were under pressure.

Prepositions of place are particularly useful because they give a visual sense of relationships.

TRY THIS

Imagine Fred.

Now imagine a table.

Now imagine Fred + table linked by different prepositions:

> *on the table*
> *under the table*
> *on top of the table*
> *at the table*
> *inside the table.*

Those tiny prepositions have a big effect!

Now try these experiments:

Note: You might like to try the "Fruit Machine" technique for this. Cut a sheet of A4 into four long strips. Write a list of words on each strip: *Names and jobs, prepositions, nouns*. Add a strip of *verbs*, if you like. Move the strips up and down to create different combinations.

TRY THIS

Imagine a place (a stream, a town, a wardrobe).

Imagine a character (a name, role or archetype).

Imagine them connected in space, using different prepositions:

> *in, about, beside, behind, below, outside, along...*

What verbs come to mind when you imagine these connections? Brainstorm a few examples.

> *The girl (walked, sat, danced, shrieked) beside the stream.*

> Sandy (searched, lay, scuttled, slumped, ate
> lunch) behind the wardrobe.

TRY THIS

Add an object into the mix. Try different prepositions to link the
following visually.

> [object] + [place]
> [character] + [object]
> [character] + [object] + [place]

With each juxtaposition of elements, you're sketching a small
word-scene.

Take your time to imagine each example. Note any you find
powerful, mysterious, or charged with something you'd like to
explore.

A strong visual image with a sense of physical presence can
provide the starting point for a story – even the central motif for
a novel or film!

TRY THIS

Look at film posters and book covers for examples of strong
images with implied prepositions. For example:

> **Jaws** – *a shark under the water*
> **Snakes on a Plane** – *snakes around a plane*
> **Silence of the Lambs** – *a moth on a woman's*
> *mouth*
> **Life of Pi** – *a man and tiger in a boat at sea*
> **The Sound of Music** – *a woman atop an*
> *Alpine meadow*
> **Parasite** – *a family by a dead person's legs*

What do these visuals make you feel? Which ones do you find
arresting? Why? How are they achieving their effects?

Now combine two or three elements to make your own posters or
book covers. Go for striking combinations.

Painting a Scene

Prepositions are very useful for sketching in a scene. Giving the reader a sense of spatial relationships helps them to build a picture in their mind's eye, and get oriented in your characters' world.

You're helping them to storyboard their own film version of your writing, right inside their head.

Now write some example sentences that could open a scene or chapter. Pay particular attention to prepositions, and where characters are in relation to each other, and their surroundings. Paint a picture for your reader.

Test them out on a friend. Can they describe the picture back to you?

This spatial clarity may not always be vital, depending on your genre, or the mood you intend to create. But it's good to be aware that although prepositions are small, familiar words, they're very powerful, and using them precisely will make a difference to the impact of your writing.

Some prepositional phrases and words are imprecise, and tend to suggest a fuzzy, lazy connection between words. If you use any of these, try substituting with a more precise word:

regarding
concerning
vis-a-vis
as regards
in terms of

Author examples

"*They had resumed their original positions, Ullman behind the desk and Jack in front of it, interviewer and interviewee, supplicant and reluctant patron.*"
    John le Carré, "*Tinker Tailor Soldier Spy*"

"*Tom and Dad strolled on the hushed earth ahead.*"
    Ray Bradbury, "*Dandelion Wine*"

"I feel their gaze like a breath on the nape of my neck, strangely without hostility but cold nevertheless."
Joanne Harris, *"Chocolat"*

"First, he pressed his hands into the springy softness of the mattress…"
Chimamanda Ngozi Adichie, *"Half of a Yellow Sun"*

"…Mrs. Pontellier also occupied her former position on the upper step, leaning listlessly against the post. Beside her was a box of bonbons, which she held out at intervals to Madame Ratignolle."
Kate Chopin, *"The Awakening"*

"The two women went away one morning to the beach together, arm in arm, under the huge white sunshade."
Kate Chopin, *"The Awakening"*

"The captain had risen earlier than usual, and set out down the beach, his cutlass swinging under the broad skirts of the old blue coat, his brass telescope under his arm, his hat tilted back upon his head."
R.L. Stevenson, *"Treasure Island"*

"…we stood watching from the front porch when Mr Radley made his final journey past our house."
Harper Lee, *"To Kill a Mockingbird"*

Prepositional Phrases

Prepositional phrases are simply groups of words that operate like prepositions. Spatial connectors like this include:

in front of
on top of
out of
ahead of
near to
up to
outside of
from under

Use them in the same way as prepositions, to explore visual, physical and spatial relationships between people, places, and things. Try also the effect of grouping prepositions together:

> *Ahead of us was a queue of lorries stretching all the way down the hill.*
>
> *Ewan jumped out from behind the curtain.*
>
> *She stretched her thin hand out from under the blanket.*
>
> *They went for a brisk walk along by the river.*

Author examples

"...spiders scattered from under the faded canvas."
    Joanne Harris, *"Chocolat"*

"Dr Reynolds parked his car in front of our house and walked to the Radleys' every time he called."
    Harper Lee, *"To Kill a Mockingbird"*

"All of a sudden, out of the middle of the trees in front of us, a thin, high, trembling voice struck up the well-known air and words: 'Fifteen men on the dead man's chest-- Yo-ho-ho and a bottle of rum!'"
    R.L. Stevenson, *"Treasure Island"*

"Finally, he climbed up and lay on top of the layers of cloth, his body curled in a tight knot."
    Chimamanda Ngozi Adichie, *"Half of a Yellow Sun"*

"Stens winked; Bud walked flank - up to the porch, gun out."
    James Ellroy, *"L.A. Confidential"*

Logic prepositions

Some prepositions and prepositional phrases connect the noun to a logical idea to show cause, purpose or reason.
    These prepositions include:

because of
due to
as a result of
in case of
owing to
for the sake of

Logical connections like this are essential for creating a coherent story, rather than just a sequence of events. This is similar thinking to E.M. Forster's famous example in *Aspects of the Novel.*[80]

> **Story:** *The king died, and then the queen died.*

> **Plot:** *The king died, and then the queen died of grief.*

Forster is illustrating a distinction between story – a sequence of events – and plot – the logic that connects them.

He could equally have used logic prepositions:

> **Plot:** *The king died, and then the queen died due to grief.*

Sometimes, these phrases can be switched for another, softer preposition:

> *Died* **due to** *grief – died* **of** *grief, died* **from** *grief*

> **In case of** *his return –* **for** *his return*

> **Due to** *a sudden flurry –* **upon** *a flurry,* **amid** *a flurry*

But it can be interesting to explore the logic of what's going on, and the different tones and nuances of these prepositions.

Some languages, such as Spanish and Japanese, express causality in a different way to English, showing a different relationship to blame or agency. For example, "the vase broke itself" suggests a gentler – more tolerant? – attitude than "she broke the vase" or "the vase got broken". Or, as happens also in English, reduced agency can be used for political reasons: "mistakes were made", "the economy collapsed", "the oil spilled into the ocean".

She left a note on the table, in case of his return, though she knew deep down he was unlikely to come back before dawn.

The party mood shrank to whispers, due to a sudden flurry of phone pings across the room.

Because of the fog, the lighthouse beam barely pierced the night, leaving the coastline invisible in the thick, swirling mist.

Author examples

"Rick appearing to be within touching distance, he was not in reality so near because of the fierce border separating our boxes."
       Kazuo Ishiguro, "Klara and the Sun"

"Because of Simon Finch's industry, Atticus was related by blood or marriage to nearly every family in the town."
       Harper Lee, "To Kill a Mockingbird"

"We'll keep him like so much gold, in case of accidents, you mark."
       R.L. Stevenson, "Treasure Island"

"Both were to be carried along with us, for the sake of safety."
       R.L. Stevenson, "Treasure Island"

TRY THIS

Create three short plot scenarios where logical connections are key. Use prepositions like *because of, due to,* or *as a result of* to introduce cause and effect. For example, "*The roads were impassible because of the storm.*" Substitute different prepositions and listen out for nuances in the viewpoint.

TRY THIS

In your close reading, find sentences with prepositional phrases and prepositions. Use word and phrase substitution to explore different meanings, and especially implications of viewpoint, agency, and responsibility. For example, *due to* can imply blame or finger-pointing, whereas *thanks to* implies a positive view. What does *as a result of* imply?

TRY THIS

Invent a conflict scenario where each side blames the other. Write a monologue for a character on each side, using prepositions and prepositional phrases to "position" their view of what happened. Next, soften the viewpoint by using causal language that is less accusatory – for example, "and then" or "thanks to" instead of "because". Then, rewrite the monologues using non-agentive language – where there's no clear agent.

"Negative" prepositions

Some prepositions and prepositional phrases indicate absence, exclusion, or a limiting condition attached to a noun. For example: *without her umbrella. **Instead of** the main road.*

These prepositions include:

> *without*
> *apart from*
> *except*
> *excluding*
> *minus*
> *outside of*
> *lacking*
> *apart from*
> *save for*
> *in place of*
> *instead of*

Mick stood apart from the crowd, watching their jostling with growing alarm.

Lacking a proper bed, she made do with an old couch and some thick blankets.

In place of a kitchen, he had a single electric ring in the middle of the floor.

What do you notice? With these prepositions, you're writing the absence, while evoking the normality. So, you're evoking two pictures at once: the rule, and the exception. This allows you to show something or someone *at odds with*, *unusual*, or *disruptive*, compared to the general status quo in that world.

These prepositions don't always have a spatial meaning – they can also be logical:

Apart from Jade, they were all signed-up members of the party.

Except for a passing pigeon, the birds he had counted were all common or garden little brown jobs.

Author examples

"Except for a heap more hair and some waiting in his eyes, he looked the way he had in Kentucky."
     Toni Morrison, "Tonight"

"He went himself to the kitchen, which was a building apart from the cottages and lying to the rear of the house."
     Kate Chopin, "The Awakening"

"Once out upon the road, Black Dog, in spite of his wound, showed a wonderful clean pair of heels, and disappeared over the edge of the hill in half a minute."
     R.L. Stevenson, "Treasure Island"

"The Radley Place fascinated Dill. In spite of our warnings and explanations it drew him as the moon draws water."
Harper Lee, "To Kill A Mockingbird"

TRY THIS

In your reading, find examples of these "negative" prepositions and phrases. Replace them with "positive" prepositions and phrases to see the effect. For example, "in spite of our warnings" becomes "thanks to our warnings". Explore how these relational words can change story and character dynamics. Consider them in relation to scene reversals and disrupting expectations.

Other Languages

In this book, we're looking at written mainstream English. But the principles apply just as well to other languages and language varieties. Using a highlighter, you can mark up text in any language, to study patterns and style.

Most languages have similar core parts of speech: nouns, verbs, adjectives, adverbs.

Many have prepositions or postpositions, showing relationships between nouns and other parts of a sentence.

Some distinctive areas in other languages include articles (or their absence), grammatical gender, cases, aspect and particles.

Some languages have unique categories or structures, such as noun classifiers based on shape or function, or politeness markers which influence verb forms.

Words also have sonic qualities, including rhythm, intonation, pitch, stress and tone.

All of these can be explored through deliberate practice!

If you're interested in digital visualization, you may be wondering how it might work with your language or language variant.

I'm a Scots speaker, and have been able to use *Textvizz* with the Scots language (see below), with some modifications.

Like many English language varieties, Scots has a rich vocabulary, and it can be hard to tell the word class from the spelling alone. This step needs context, so software designed for mainstream English can struggle a bit. And actually, language classification isn't an exact science, and humans can find it tricky, too! *Textvizz* lets you modify the basic visual to add or remove anything you want to.

Whether you write in a regional or cultural dialect, one of the many kinds of World English, or an entirely different language, you can still use deliberate practice to build your skills.

When chapmen billies leave the street,
And drouthy neibors, neibors meet,
As market days are wearing late,
An' folk begin to tak the gate;
While we sit bousing at the nappy,
And getting fou and unco happy,
We think na on the lang Scots miles,
The mosses, waters, slaps, and styles,
That lie between us and our hame,
Where sits our sulky sullen dame.
Gathering her brows like gathering storm,
Nursing her wrath to keep it warm.

Scots language poem by Robert Burns, parsed by *Textvizz*.

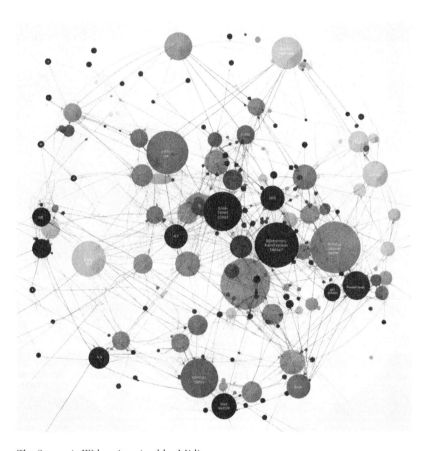

The Semantic Web as imagined by Midjourney.

Part 6

Shape & Pattern

Foregrounding

In writing, *foregrounding* means making certain elements stand out from the others. For example, you'll probably want to draw your reader's attention to the arrival of a significant new character, plot development, or murder weapon. The background weather, underfoot greenery or stained curtains in the drawing room probably aren't as important, in the scheme of things.

There are many ways to pull focus in writing. The main point to recognise is that human only have so much focus. We can only handle so much cognitive load. So skilled writers draw attention to chosen focal points, by sculpting and shaping their writing, whether through rhythm, vocabulary choice, use of space, novelty, surprise, sound, and other techniques.

Signal-to-noise ratio

A helpful analogy for foregrounding is the radio terminology of *signal versus noise.*

Signal is useful noise – the kind you want to come across clearly.

Noise is the background noise – the static, crackles and atmospherics which add to the overall effect, but aren't the emphasis you want.

Note that *signal-to-noise* doesn't judge sounds as being intrinsically valuable or not. Rather, there are sounds you want more of, and sounds you want less of, depending on your goal.

For example, if someone you've recorded has mouth clicks in their voice, it's very useful to hear just the clicks, so you can do something about them.

This non-judging way of looking at sound is helpful for writing, because words aren't intrinsically good or bad. It depends what you want to achieve.

A good signal-to-noise ratio means enough focus on what's important – the signal – and other sound – noise – turned down so that the signal comes through clearly.

With a poor signal-to-noise ratio, the signal is obscured by the noise, and the effect is muddy, or even downright incomprehensible.

When it comes to writing, you need plenty of *signal* relative to *noise*. Then, your intention is clear. Melody cuts through clearly. Voices are salient and attract attention. The murder weapon isn't lost in a clutter of objects competing for attention.

So how do you use this in your writing?

First, it may be helpful to know a little about the psychology of human concentration and focus, and its limitations.

Short-term memory

If you've ever struggled to remember long phone numbers, you'll be aware of the limitations of your short-term memory. A famous psychology study[81] worked out that we can retain around seven items in our short-term memory at any one time. Actually, it's seven *plus or minus two*, so for some of us, it's only *five* items. Quite a thought!

More recent research[82] suggests that number might be closer to *four* plus or minus two, taking account of "chunking". Memory athletes often use the technique of grouping related items together in chunks, to remember them better.

For example, this string of 12 objects is hard to remember. Give it a try:

elephant, guitar, pineapple, kangaroo, telescope, octopus, bicycle, giraffe, umbrella, dragon, castle, lighthouse.

Now, let's group them into three categories: animals, objects, fantasy-related. Now, it's easier:

elephant, kangaroo, octopus, giraffe; guitar, pineapple, telescope, bicycle, umbrella; dragon, castle, lighthouse.

Another memory tactic is to enhance the images with vivid mental pictures and associations:

a giraffe playing the guitar, a dragon with a telescope at the top of a lighthouse…

Stickability of vivid images is good news for imaginative writers. But even with this clever chunking, the limitation for short-term memory is still four plus or minus one items. So, your readers may struggle to recall all the details that are so significant for you as the writer.

That's just short-term memory. So how does it get into longer-term memory? Through *encoding* and *retrieval*. Brain processing transforms your sensory input, so that it can be stored and recalled. Repetition is a key part of this.

An important takeaway for writers and long-term memory recall is that information has to be actively maintained, or it gets lost.

So, your beloved character who appears in Chapter One, disappears, and only returns in Chapter Nine, won't be remembered.

Similarly, the yellow scarf described on page 20 when you introduce your heroine might not ring a bell when it turns up in a hotel room on page 50. It has essentially vanished from view.

Any important prop or plot device needs to be kept alive with small reminders, or "touches", now and again.

The same is true of place description, character appearance or minor characters in scenes. If we only hear once that they're up a mountain, with a dog, wearing orange jackets that will later be used to find them after an avalanche, we won't remember. We need repeated "touches" or touchpoints to help our recall.

Think of a firefly whose light fades into darkness. Set it glowing again, and the trail will stay alive.

These might be as simple as repeating a name or pronoun now and again, to keep the character visible for the reader.

Bearing in mind *signal-to-noise-ratio* and *short-term memory*, not everything can be equally important. Choose carefully what needs to be most salient, and reinforce those aspects with subtle *touches*.

Character names

Names are an effective way to keep characters present in the reader's mind, as long as this feels natural and isn't overdone.

Like all words, names and their sounds evoke mind-pictures, and so too many names with a similar length and sound can be confusing. For example, the names *Bert, Bill* and *Brian* conjure men of a similar age, class and geography, so they're hard to distinguish.

It's better to make major character names more salient, by giving them distinct sounds and associations. *Russell, Zac* and *Mr Austin* are a lot easier to keep separate in your mind.

Characters without names

What about secondary characters who don't have names? Say they're extras, or have a peripheral role – how do you keep them in view for the reader?

Earlier, I mentioned Stephen King's technique of describing characters with a striking visual the first time they're mentioned. This then becomes their nickname. In these examples, the characters are anonymous and being watched at a distance, by a third person narrator.

The guy in the Mister Softee truck…

Mister Softee Guy…

The woman in the power suit…

Power Suit Woman…

The two girls had exactly the same haircut… (one) was blond and her friend was brunette; they were Pixie Light and Pixie Dark.
        Stephen King, "Cell"

Note that King uses slight variation to keep the flame alive. He avoids constant repetition, which could quickly get dull.

In a similar way, you can write touches in slightly different language each time.

The man in the tattered shirt…

His ragged shirt…

He tore off the last shreds of his shirt…

Beware of tipping over into a style known as elegant variation. This is when alternative words are used to describe the same thing, to demonstrate rhetorical and poetic skill or nuance – and also to avoid repetition. For example:

The dog chased the cat. Then the dog caught the cat.

The dog chased the cat, and then the animal caught its prey.

The second sentence illustrates an elegant variation of the first.

In some language cultures, this rhetorical style is encouraged as a hallmark of good style. In English, it can be confusing or distracting.

Fowler's *A Dictionary of Modern English Usage*[83] advises against elegant variation.

TRY THIS

Choose three or four key attributes to describe your characters. What's their signature visual? Sound? Scent, if they have one? Voice quality? Manner or habit? Now describe each of these, using similar language or close synonyms (as in *tattered* shirt, *ragged*, *shredded*). Next, translate these descriptions into related verbs, nouns, adjectives. Write sentences evoking the character, without repeating the same words or phrases.

TRY THIS

Imagine a scene where a character and animal are hiding, while someone is in the same room, doing something they shouldn't. Say, Zac and Skippy the dog are behind a curtain, while a police officer ransacks the office. Write the scene, using their names. Then rewrite it, using other ways to refer to the characters. For example, a wet nose and low growl might evoke the dog, without using its name.

Good Words, Right Order

The order of information within sentences and paragraphs can make a big difference to readers' comprehension.

Sometimes, you'll want to keep words back, and "land" them at the end of a sentence, for maximum impact – a bit like a cinematic reveal, or landing a joke punchline. Other times, you'll want to make sure the reader is clearly oriented, by including significant information at the start.

Compare these sentences, for example:

> *They found a rusting knife covered in blood in the last drawer of Smiley's desk.*

> *The search lasted for hours. It wasn't until they reached the last drawer of Smiley's desk that they finally found what they were looking for: a bloody, rusty knife.*

When they searched Smiley's desk, they finally found what they were looking for: a rusty kitchen knife covered in blood.

Each of these approaches has a different rhythm, and creates a different emotional effect, by emphasising different words through their placement.

The first example has the gory murder weapon buried inside the sentence, making its presence sound factual, almost casual. The desk, in end position, sounds more significant.

The second example lands firstly on "hours", emphasising the epic search. The second sentence delays the weapon reveal, almost savouring the moment, by using a convoluted negative structure: "it wasn't until… that". The sentences ends with a lingering look at the gory knife. This gives the sentences an extra performative quality, a dramatic rise and fall.

The third example is somewhere between, landing dramatically on the word "blood", which then has space to resound.

Read each example aloud. Which one do you prefer?

There isn't a right or wrong answer here – just different approaches and rhythms. I find the first one very flat, with nothing really salient apart from the final landing on "desk".

As a quick reader, I might well miss the fly-by appearance of the murder weapon.

I've often read student writer drafts with this issue, where important nuggets are hidden inside flat sentences, and minor elements occupy powerful real estate at the end.

Greater control of how information unfolds can make important words more salient. This makes all the difference to a reader's comprehension and experience.

TRY THIS

Rewrite this sentence in three different ways, bringing out what you see as the important elements for the story:

As the storm raged outside, filling the night with flashes of lightning and peals of thunder, the old lighthouse keeper discovered a hidden door beneath the floorboards.

Did you find this straightforward? Was it easy to come up with two or three examples?

If not, here's a breakdown of process steps to try:

Firstly, what's the story?

News journalists have to do this all the time: read a long chunk of text and extract the story. If you had to write a headline, what would it be?

Probably something like:

> *Lighthouse man discovers hidden door.*

This cuts to the chase. Yes, there's a storm raging outside. Yes, it's a wild, dark night, with thunder and lighting assaulting the old man's senses.

But the key story point is the one you'd tell your friends down the pub.

> *"Wow! Guess what happened next! This old man,*
> *right, scrabbling about on the floor, in the dark, storm*
> *ranging all around… and – get this: he finds a hidden*
> *door!"*

This may seem obvious, but it's worth digging into, as it highlights techniques of salience, withholding, and generally controlling your reader's attention – the difference between simply writing down the facts, and writing with clarity, purpose and style.

And by the way, the "down the pub" question is absolutely taught in journalism as a way to think about story. *What's new? What's exciting? What will catch the attention of your audience of friends?*

Another way to pinpoint what's important is to highlight the nouns. This excellent actor's technique was introduced to me by a director friend. He taught Shakespeare to first-time actors, who often struggled with the unfamiliar language and rhythms.

"Emphasise the nouns", he said. "These are important for understanding. If you land the nouns, you'll get the gist across."

Use a highlighter or Word highlighting and try this for yourself.

> *As the storm raged outside, filling the night with flashes of lightning and peals of thunder, the old lighthouse keeper discovered a hidden door beneath the floorboards.*

Here's how it looks in my app, *Textvizz*:

> As the storm raged outside, filling the night with flashes of lightning and peals of thunder, the old lighthouse keeper discovered a hidden door beneath the floorboards.

Read the sentence aloud, emphasizing the nouns. Try it as a performer! Notice how the rapid rush of "storm" words gives you the chance to evoke the turbulence with your voice. But it's still hard to emphasise the crucial *door*, because it's undermined by the trailing *floorboards*, which are far less exciting.

Also, from the lighthouse keeper's viewpoint, they'd appear *before* the door (*scrabble on floorboards > notice unusual feature > find door*). So the floorboards feel in the wrong place logically, as well as rhythmically. This distracts from the reader's immersion in the story world.

Try putting the floorboards before the door, to build tension (*withholding > release* technique).

Then, try a full stop after *door*. Next, backflip in time, beginning a new paragraph with the floorboards (*landing > backflip* technique).

Notice that these two approaches deal with time in different ways.

So, you've now explored the impact of nouns, landing, and order of information.

What about verbs?

Although my director friend didn't discuss this, verbs can carry just as much weight. After all, verbs are action words, so you'd expect them to create momentum in the story.

TRY THIS

Highlight the verbs of the same sentence, and read it aloud, emphasising the verbs:

As the storm raged outside, filling the night with flashes of lightning and peals of thunder, the old lighthouse keeper discovered a hidden door beneath the floorboards.

As the storm `raged` outside, `filling` the night with flashes of lightning and peals of thunder, the old lighthouse keeper `discovered` a hidden door beneath the floorboards.

What do you discover? *Raged* feels good to say – full of tension, and a long vowel you can really get stuck into. *Filling* isn't great – not exactly powerful and percussive, compared with the thunderous surroundings. *Discovered* feels relatively flimsy, with short vowels that aren't ideal for projecting. It also feels like a gentle process of some duration, rather than a single decisive action of a moment, as in:

*I **discovered** the Holy Grail (while I was visiting Rome last year).*

Whereas a single action would probably use a different verb, less abstract, more physical:

*I **uncovered** the Holy Grail (which shone with an unearthly light).*

*I **unveiled** the Holy Grail.*

*Shaking, I **lifted** the Holy Grail.*

So, bearing these thoughts about nouns and verbs in mind, here are further examples for rewriting.

As you try this, think about the *story* word, order of information, landing, and breaking up sentences to control pace and salience. Remember that beginnings and endings are impactful.

146

Beneath the bustling city streets lay a network of tunnels leading to an ancient treasure guarded by mythical creatures.

In the middle of the night, while everyone was asleep, the fire alarm suddenly went off, causing panic throughout the building.

In the library, surrounded by the scent of old books and the soft glow of the lamps, she came upon a letter that revealed her true past.

Context, Detail

When it comes to information, people usually find it easier to take in context first, then detail.

That's because it's easier to remember something that fits into your existing knowledge framework. It's anchored to the framework, like a jigsaw piece that you can easily place, because of what's already there.

A single jigsaw piece is free-floating. You don't know where it belongs, until you find clues to click it into the bigger picture.

For example, let's say you come across a *blorft*. You've no idea whether it's animal, vegetable, mineral, place, planet, particle, or spiritual being. But if you know it's an ingredient in Norwegian traditional cooking (it isn't! – it's made up), you can categorise it under "food", and have a better chance of remembering it.

I was interested to discover that sign languages used by people with hearing impairment also use a *context-before-detail* or *topic-comment* structure. This makes it easier to understand quickly and efficiently, and is in marked contrast to the *subject-verb-object* order typical of spoken English.

Here are some structure examples from American Sign Language (ASL) and British Sign Language (BSL), with their mainstream English equivalents:

English: I'm going to the park tomorrow.

ASL: Tomorrow, park, I go.

BSL: Tomorrow, park, me go.

English: My sister is studying in the library.

ASL: Library, my sister study.

BSL: Library, my sister, study.

Notice that these sign languages establish space and time context early on, before describing specific actions.

Radio writing also typically sketches in context, before going into detail.

Although fiction writers have different freedoms, it's good to know about this natural cognitive tendency, and use it when it's useful.

Scene setting and background information aren't mere descriptive passages or pace-stalling asides. They're crucial for guiding readers through the narrative.

Author examples

"One may as well begin with Jerome's e-mails to his father: To: HowardBelsey_@fas.Wellington.edu From: Jeromeabroad@easymail.com Date: 5 November Subject: Hey, Dad"
      Zadie Smith, "On Beauty"

"It was a quiet morning, the town covered over with darkness and at ease in bed. Summer gathered in the weather, the wind had the proper touch, the breathing of the world was long and warm and slow. You had only to rise, lean from your window, and know that this indeed was the first real time of freedom and living, this was the first morning of summer. Douglas Spaulding, twelve, freshly wakened, let summer idle him on its early-morning stream."
      Ray Bradbury, "Dandelion Wine"

Sentence Beginnings and Ends

The beginnings and ends of sentences and paragraphs are powerful real estate in your writing.

Words with space around them are more salient. Think of the effect of a pause in music, or white space in visual art. They create room for their neighbour to stand out, for fresh impetus. The space can be tiny, but it still creates patterns, and ebb and flow.

TRY THIS

Try clapping in regular groups of eight, with a hard clap on each first beat. Then try the same clapping sequence, missing out the fifth beat. Then, the second beat. Notice how one tiny space completely changes the feeling of the rhythm. The bounce of hiphop and syncopation of jazz, and their great rhythmic complexity, are made from exactly this kind of playing with small spaces between sounds.

Rhyming poetry and stage writing make much use of line endings. Performers work with "landing" a word or a joke.

Musicians work with the attack and decay of musical notes and phrases. Sound engineers use an "envelope" shape to describe the shape of notes – the *ADSR* envelope, which stands for *attack, decay, sustain, release*. Each note can be shown in terms of how it starts and ends, and its duration.

A note might be short and sharp, creating a lot of sudden impact – think: a single loud drumbeat.

Or, it might insinuate itself gradually, build over a long period, and then gradually fade to nothing – think: a distant band playing, coming closer, passing by into the distance.

ADSR typically applies to single notes and sounds, but the metaphor of attack, decay, sustain, release can equally be applied to longer durations – phrases and melodies.

From there, it's only a short step to thinking about the shape and effects of sentences.

Just as musicians use attack and decay for the beginnings and ends of phrases, you as a prose writer can do this, too.

Speak this sentence aloud a few times – the famous opening of *Rebecca* by Daphne du Maurier.

> *Last night I dreamt I went to Manderley again.*[84]

Listen to the rise and fall of the sounds, peaking at *Manderley*, and falling away at *again*.

To me, this reads as a poetic line, almost iambic, with a pattern of stressed and unstressed syllables. It has some of the qualities we've looked at previously – the context setting of *last night*, the clear viewpoint of *I*, the evocative place-name, and the dreamlike decaying of *again*.

It has other lovely sonic qualities – *dreamt-went*, *night-went*, and the sonorous name of Manderley itself.

Beginnings and endings have a big job to do. You also need to manage transitions. Again, music analogies can be helpful.

Here's an ending example from Hilary Mantel's *Wolf Hall* – the end of Chapter One.

> "... *He will remember his first sight of the open sea: a grey wrinkled vastness, like the residue of a dream.*"

Read it aloud a couple of times.

Mantel leaves readers with an evocative image, and a space for their own dreaming.

Then, Chapter Two picks up with a fresh attack:

> "*So: Stephen Gardiner. Going out, as he's coming in.*"

Short phrases, the storyteller's "so", a new character, no messing about. An authoritative storyteller launches us into the new chapter.

Using deliberate practice to look at transition examples by different authors can help you to uncover effective strategies.

But when you find a pattern that works for you, don't overdo it! A rise-fall cadence can quickly become repetitive. Putting landing words at the end of sentences can also become repetitive. Short, sharp pick-up can also become a musical tic in your writing.

I've sometimes spotted student writers overusing patterns such as *-ing* clause at the start of a sentence:

> *Glancing over her shoulder, she quickened her pace.*

> *Clutching the letter, he sat down by the window.*

These sentences on their own are fine, but the same rise and fall repeated every other paragraph will soon get tired.

Make sure you ring the changes, and keep the flow of your writing moving and alive.

TRY THIS

Play with musical patterns. Try putting significant nouns at the end of long and short sentences.

> *It was dark as they made their way up the drive.*

> *She rummaged around in the handbag, past the files and folders, phone, keys, tattered tissues, leaking pens, crumbs, dust, glitter, and there, in a fold of lining, found the knife.*

See the effect of one, two and three-syllable words at the end, eg *dream, pencil, attitude, remembering.*

Read some lines of poetry to see how words might be used at the ends of lines. Look out for *stressed* and *unstressed* syllables at the ends of lines – sometimes called "masculine" and "feminine" endings.

Here's an example from *The Raven* by Edgar Allan Poe.[85]

> *While I nodded, nearly napping, suddenly there came a tapping, (unstressed ending)*

> *As of someone gently rapping, rapping at my chamber door. (stressed ending)*

151

TRY THIS

Choose some sentences from your work in progress – perhaps some from a fast-paced section, some from a slower, atmospheric section. Experiment with the words at the end of your sentences, by substituting single and multisyllable words, stressed and unstressed endings, concrete and abstract words. What kinds of impact and mood do these changes evoke?

Colour

Research suggests that colour words are often more memorable than other kinds of words. This may be because they have strong visual and emotional associations.

It's thought several effects are in play here. Colour words are more distinctive and easier to visualise than abstract or neutral words. The Von Restorff[86] effect shows that distinct and different content is more salient than what's around it. So, colours may feel more salient in a sentence.

It's also thought that information processed in two ways – verbal and non-verbal – can enhance memory and recall. This is known as the Dual Coding Theory[87]. The idea is that language that uses two modes of brain activity – say, visual and aural – is more memorable, as the brain has dual ways to reconstruct it.

This idea is often used in education, where illustrations and colours can help to reinforce written text – and the other way round.

It suggests that writing that evokes visuals such as colour, along with sounds or other senses, may be easier to engage with, and more memorable. This may also be why techniques such as metaphor – with a clear central image – create powerful impact.

Author examples

> "Mrs Pontellier's eyes were quick and bright; they were a yellowish brown, about the color of her hair."
> Kate Chopin, "The Awakening"

"Dill was a curiosity. He wore blue linen shorts that buttoned to his shirt, his hair was snow white and stuck to his head like duck-fluff; he was a year my senior but I towered over him."

Harper Lee, "To Kill a Mockingbird"

"There was the big man with red hair, whose name he always forgot, sitting at a table with a blonde girl. The red-haired man waved a hand, and Tom's hand went up limply in response."

Patricia Highsmith, "The Talented Mr Ripley"

"I remember him as if it were yesterday, as he came plodding to the inn door, his sea-chest following behind him in a hand-barrow; a tall, strong, heavy, nut-brown man; his tarry pig-tail falling over the shoulders of his soiled blue coat; his hands ragged and scarred, with black, broken nails, and the saber cut across one cheek, a dirty, livid white."

R.L. Stevenson, "Treasure Island"

TRY THIS

Brainstorm some metaphors for your book or project in progress. Pick examples from different kinds of world – *work, sport, leisure, food, the natural world*. Which seems most memorable and best aligned, to you? Try your ideas with different colours. What's the emotional impact for you, and potentially your audience (bearing in mind that colours vary in cultural significance)? If you were designing the film poster, what would be on it? Try designing a simple poster – even a scratchy drawing to capture the essence. If this drawing works for you, use it as a touchstone when you're writing.

153

Active engagement

People who read are already actively engaging with writing. The act of reading is a form of decoding, and requires a level of cognitive effort. It can't be absorbed directly, without thinking.

Some other art forms, such as film or TV, need less cognitive effort. They're more aligned to the experience of everyday life, offering a mix of visual and auditory stimulus that we can react to without necessarily thinking. Think of a sudden loud bang on TV, or a monster looming at you in a cinema. Visuals and audio can connect directly with our senses and create emotional effects, without the need for decoding.

In some ways, the act of reading means absorbing words to activate your own internal film show, complete with special effects, emotional impact and intriguing stories. Reading already creates a sense of immersiveness, described as "the fictive dream" by novelist and literary critic John Gardner.[88]

But how can you actively make your writing more engaging? How can you draw readers in, beyond the basic necessary skills of clear, expressive writing?

In theatre, writers use many proven techniques to encourage active engagement by audiences. These draw on universal human traits, and are helpful for authors in any genre.

If you'd like to explore this, you'll find these techniques covered in my book, *Dramatic Techniques for Creative Writers*.[89] They include the use of objects, physicalisation, transformation, fourth wall, reversals, status, and many more creative concepts that can be applied to any writing discipline.

Rhythm and Sound

Even as tiny children, we feel the joys of rhythm and sound in writing. Children's tales and nursery rhymes are full of playful sound patterns, repetitions, funny, memorable character names.

Old MacDonald had a farm, E-I-E-I-O...

I do not like green eggs and ham.

I do not like them, Sam-I-am.

I do not like them here or there.

I do not like them anywhere.[90]

Pippi Longstocking, Moominpappa, Moominmamma, Mymble, Groke, Snork Maiden...

These sounds have a heightened effect, making the characters more salient and memorable within the story.

TRY THIS

Choose a range of books by authors in the genre you're writing in. Make a list of protagonist and antagonist names. What sound qualities do they have? What vowels and consonants do they use? How many syllables do they have? Where does the stress fall? Brainstorm new names with similar qualities. Substitute different rhythms, stresses, sounds. How does this affect tone, emotional impact, or even genre?

Addition, Subtraction

In the world of sculpture, artists often refer to "additive" and "subtractive" ways of working. In the *additive* process, the artist will join together or compile several pieces of material. In the *subtractive* process, they *remove* pieces of material, whether by carving, cutting, sanding, or some other method.

We've already looked at how writing works at different scales – story structure, chapter, paragraph, sentence, chunk, phrase, and individual words and letters.

You can use additive and subtractive thinking at any of these levels. If you tend to overwrite and cut out extraneous words, you're subtracting. If you underwrite – say, leave out vital plot points, or don't provide enough detail to bring characters and worlds to life – then you're doing additive editing.

Depending on the kind of writer you are, you'll find your editing process instinctively involves both, at different times.

In my case, at sentence level, particularly in scripts, I typically overwrite. In performance writing, less is more! So, editing at this level is a process of cutting out words, paring back, to let the nuggets shine through.

When it comes to story or scene level, I usually find things missing, or underwritten, and need to expand them.

Maybe I've lost sight of a specific character, and need to add a few "touches" to keep them alive in the scene for the reader. Or, I've discovered a story point that needs a clue "planted" earlier, to create a later "payoff". This is a good editing pass to carry out at a later stage of your editing process. It helps to tighten the weave of the story.

Additive and subtractive thinking can also be used in a playful way, to experiment and expand your writing toolkit. There are lots of ways to do this – by this point, you have the tools to work out your own.

Maybe your characters are a bit flat, and can't be clearly "seen"? Or they feel a bit wooden, like puppets moving around? Use deliberate practice: Find some examples of writing by authors whose characters you love. Close-read, and work out how they're achieving their effects. What specific words help to paint pictures? When they "speak", what words make you relate to them? Can you describe what these words are? If they're verbs, are they active, or passive? What senses do they evoke? If they're nouns: abstract or concrete? Adjectives: colours? Shapes? Scale? Texture?

Then, gather your own examples. Think through how you express the same ideas in your own language, your own distinct world. How might your friends or family express the same idea?

Over time, this process will help you to get more sensitized to language, and prime your radar for spotting useful techniques.

For another additive experiment, start from language itself. This will get you exploring word use from the ground up, looking closely at words, and what they do. It might sound basic, but it's incredibly helpful, and fascinating!

I find it strange that studying language use is so often the domain of linguistics, rather than literature and creative writing. Writers can learn so much about style through linguistics, especially literary stylistics, which looks at style and its effects. Deliberate practice helps you to get a taster of stylistics by focusing on the writers and craft aspects you want to learn from.

TRY THIS

First, write a short, simple sentence. Then expand it in different ways.

For example:

The cat sat on the mat.

Add qualifiers such as adjectives and adverbs.

Add negatives (*not, never, un-*).

Add modal verbs (*can, could, may, might, should, will, would...*).

Add *which* clauses (a *clause* is a group of words containing a subject and verb).

Add *and, but, or* clauses.

Add proper names in place of nouns.

Read your sentences aloud. Look out for anything that jumps out as unexpected, or a disruption, provocation or conflict. Could it inspire a story?

Fruit Machine

The Fruit Machine technique is a way to generate lots of combinations, whether for inspiration, or to explore word combinations that gel, jar or surprise in different ways. It's a bit like using colour strips to see how colours "play" with each other. Do they crackle with excitement or disruption? Do they feel familiar, as though they belong together? Do they feel melodious, rhythmic, dissonant, awkward, evocative?

TRY THIS

Cut a sheet of A4 into four long strips. Write a list of words on each strip: *Names and jobs, prepositions, nouns, verbs*. Include other parts of speech you want to play with. Move the strips up and down to create different combinations.

How you use this is up to you – try your own creative combinations!

Some ideas to start with:

Change the order of words in a sentence.

Explore abstract nouns vs concrete nouns.

Use a noun strip in place of verbs.

Use a verb strip in place of nouns.

Add a strip for *-un, not, never* and other negative words.

Blackout Technique

Blackout technique is a fun way to generate ideas by exploring texts with the help of a Sharpie marker pen.

TRY THIS

To do this, print a page from a newspaper or book. It may be easiest to do this by taking a photo of the publication with a mobile phone, and printing it out. The page can be meaningful to you, or not.

You're going to make a visual poem, using the words as your treasure trove.

Use the Sharpie to black out the words you don't want.

Do it quickly! Don't overthink it, have fun, and see what playful ideas your subconscious brings up.

The result will look like a top-secret redacted document, with only a few words left visible around the page.

For inspiration, see poet Austin Kleon's book, *Newspaper Blackout*.[91]

Oulipo Experiments

Oulipo is an avant-garde French literary group with an interest in experiments based on their own devised rules. It was founded in 1960 by Raymond Queneau, and is still running today.

The name "Oulipo" is short for *Ouvroir de Littérature Potentielle* (Workshop of Potential Literature).

Oulipo use rules to generate new kinds of text, rejecting chance and the subconscious as an approach to literary creativity. Their rigorous experiments, inspired by mathematics and puzzles, produce inventive results which have exploded their thinking beyond the usual confines of language. Notable members of Oulipo included Italo Calvino[92] and Georges Perec.[93]

TRY THIS

To get started with Oulipo-style techniques, invent a rule, and apply it to a text.

Here are some suggestions:

Snowball. Write a poem where each line has one more syllable – or one more word – than the previous line.

Pointless constraint. Write a story in exactly 50 words.

Word ladder. Write a piece where each new sentence changes a word from the previous sentence. With each change, the sentence still has to make sense.

N+7. Here, *N* stands for *noun,* and *+7* means *seven words later.* Take an existing short text, and replace all the nouns with the seventh noun after it in the dictionary.

Lipogram. Write a short text without using a chosen letter.[94]

Net Bags

This section goes in detail into relative clauses and structural frames that can be infinitely extended. I call these "net bags", because they can act as containers for other words.

I feel this is important as an antidote to the traditional dictionary-oriented approach to language, which foregrounds individual words. Given that research shows most people speak in clusters and saccades of words, it's worth considering the limitations and possibilities of these and other longer structures.[95]

Words that join groups of words together do a lot of heavy lifting in terms of creating sustained, expansive sentences, and longer rhythms.

There are two main kinds of joining or linking words: *conjunctions* (easy to remember because it includes the word *junction*); and relative pronouns, such as *which, who, whom, that, whose, where, when,* and *why.*

Conjunctions are so familiar that you might not be tuned in to their importance. They play a crucial part in sentence logic. For a discussion of these, see **Part 5: Language Topics**.

Now for a deep-dive into a crucial net bag in language – the relative clause.

Relative clause

What's a relative clause? You can often spot them by looking out for words like which, where, who, that, especially in the middle of a sentence. They modify a noun, like this:

> *The cat which…*
> *The red house where…*
> *The man who…*
> *The storm that…*

Which, where, who, whom, that… these clauses provide additional information about the noun.

They're like a mini loop of added information – an aside, if you like. Or an embedded nugget. Then the main sentence picks up and moves on.

> *The cat which sat on the mat had had enough.*

> *The cat, which sat on the mat, had had enough.*[96]

A relative clause creates a span between the noun and its main verb.

> *The cat (…) had had enough.*

Other words used to introduce relative clauses include a group of relative pronouns: *where, who, whom, whose, that.*

Relative pronouns? *Pro-nouns* means words that stand *for* the noun. They're a kind of shorthand – like using *M* as a shorthand for a first name: *M. Monroe.*

> *The cat which sat…*

Here's the sentence without the pronoun:

> *The cat – meaning the specific cat sitting on the mat – was getting impatient.*

> *The cat which sat on the mat prowled closer to the mousehole.*

The main point here is that relative clauses are expandable, and a great way to tuck in chunks of information, while still moving the story on.

How expandable? Let's expand the *which* clause.

> *The cat which sat on the mat, licking its paws, bored to tears…*

> *The cat which sat on the mat, licking its paws, combing its fur, bored to tears…*

> *…had had enough.*

That's a long gap between the cat and its main verb, *had had enough.* It just about works.

But in theory, a *which* clause is infinitely expandable.

> *The cat, which sat on the mat, licking its paws, bored
> to tears, wondering how long it would be till that
> wretched human returned from work, bestowed some
> ineffectual cuddles and opened the ghastly tin of ghastly
> goo masquerading as food, **had had enough**.*

In theory, infinitely expandable. In practice, try reading aloud and breathing. If you run out of breath, the sentence or its clauses might need a rework.

The playwright Simon Gray, author of the memoir *The Smoking Diaries*,[97] uses this kind of clause for great comic effect, with long, conversational sentences that show him wrestling with everyday challenges. Here's an example in his style:

> *"I sat at my desk, which was cluttered with papers from
> last week's meeting, thinking about the letter, which I
> still hadn't written, that would explain everything."*

It's even possible to nest relative clauses inside each other, like Russian dolls. After all, every noun has the potential to be expanded.

Here's an example of nested relative clauses – don't worry, it won't go on infinitely:

> *The cat, which sat on the mat, licking her paws,
> **which** were bloodied from her battle with Rex, **which**
> hadn't gone well, wondering how long it would be
> till that wretched human returned from its office,
> **which** was somewhere north of Edinburgh, bestowed
> some ineffectual cuddles, **which** totally triggered her
> itchy spots, and opened the ghastly tin of ghastly goo
> masquerading as food, **which** had no nutritional value
> whatsoever, **had had enough**.*

The effect is of an escalating cat-rant which finally resolves when the main verb lands – with a bump, with a sense of relief: *had had enough.*

Each noun has a loop, with its own little burst of explanation or background information.

Why is this important? Because relative clauses are *everywhere*.

And they're great for including background information, while also keeping the flow going.

For grammar lovers

As a writer, you don't need to know about the definitions that follow. They're added for anyone who wants a bit more information, and might help you with comma use.

And it's important to remember that language doesn't always fit into a single category – it can fit more than one at the same time. Also, our intention can shift under us as we write or speak. Or, you may want to use ambiguity as a hallmark of your style.

Those caveats aside, here's an overview of relative clauses.

There are two main kinds of relative clause: *defining*, and *non-defining*.

With *defining* relative clauses, the extra information in the clause is essential to the noun. It provides a *definition* of the noun. Without that information, the sentence wouldn't make sense.

Sometimes, it's called a *restrictive* relative clause. *The cat, artist, car…* is restricted to that *particular* cat, artist, car.

> *The woman who called is my friend.*

> *The artist whose painting you loved is well-known in France.*

> *The dog that bit me belongs to my brother.*

In other words, the *specific* dog.

Note that *that* is a special case. It's used only in defining relative clauses, and doesn't have commas.

With non-defining relative clauses, the extra information isn't essential. If you cut it, the sentence still makes sense. This kind of clause usually has commas around it.

> *My brother, who lives in New York, is visiting us next week.*

> *The red car, which is parked outside, belongs to my neighbour.*

Thinking of "by the way" or "aside" can help here.

> *My brother, who by the way lives in New York, is visiting us next week.*
>
> *The red car, which by the way is parked outside, belongs to my neighbour.*

TRY THIS

Consider these examples of *non-defining* relative clauses.

> *The red car, which is parked outside, belongs to my neighbour.*
>
> *My youngest brother, who by the way lives in New York, is visiting us next week.*

Rewrite the relative clauses to create new sentences.

> *The red car, which is parked outside, belongs to my neighbour.*
>
> *My youngest brother, who's an IT consultant, is visiting us next week.*
>
> *My youngest brother, whose wife has started a new job, is visiting us next week.*

Now, experiment with combinations of nouns and relative pronouns (*which, whose, who, whom, where*).

TRY THIS

Consider these examples of *defining* relative clauses.

> *The red car that's parked outside belongs to my neighbour.*
>
> *My brother who lives in New York is visiting us next week.*

In the first example, it's the specific red car parked outside that belongs to the neighbour. It's not a "by the way" or "aside".

164

I typically use *that* when I'm speaking. It feels more conversational and informal. *Which* feels more formal. I'd probably use it in written English, especially as a British English speaker. *That* is used more often by American English speakers.

Think about your own cultural and social background, and what you use when you're speaking, writing, together with friends or coworkers. Write some examples of *that* and *which* clauses for these different situations.

How might you use this for different characters?

TRY THIS

Find examples of relative clauses in your reading by published authors (look for relative pronouns: *which, whose, who, that*...). Ideally, choose a paragraph with several relative pronouns. Highlight the nouns and main verbs. Then, highlight the relative pronouns in a different colour:

> *The red car, which is parked outside, belongs to my neighbour.*

Decide whether the relative clauses are defining or non-defining. Sometimes, commas can help.

Read the sentences aloud. Decide whether the clause feels like an aside, or a definition.

TRY THIS

Look for relative clause examples with different kinds of noun: abstract (*hope, freedom, metaphor*); collective (*flock, bouquet, suite, team*), and names of people and places.

Write your own sentences inspired by what you find.

Artificial Intelligence (AI)

AI is a controversial topic for creatives. Generative writing engines such as ChatGPT are evolving so fast that it's impossible to keep up.

Some creatives find AI developments threatening, others are happily using AI tools. Others refuse to use AI for various good reasons, including energy use by AI computer servers.

However, even if you've not tried standalone AI apps such as ChatGPT, you may find you're using it anyway, without realising, as it's often baked into more familiar products such as Adobe Creative Cloud, Grammarly, and search engines such as Bing. It has been predicted that it will displace the current main search engine, Google, as a search tool. I certainly find it more useful than search engines for some kinds of learning, which I'll go into shortly.

Whatever your views on AI, there's no doubt that it's transforming the creative landscape and creative livelihoods, and is here to stay.

So, it makes sense to get familiar with what AI can do for writers, so that you're aware of it, even if you don't go on to use it.

AI is developing so fast that it's becoming increasingly hard to detect. Artists have been accused of using AI for their handcrafted work. I recently ran a mix of AI-generated and real photos of people past a friend, and was astonished to find that not only were they unable to identify AI images –they also identified real photos as AI creations. This for me was a turning-point.

An aside, in case you're curious: I haven't used AI to generate the writing in this book. I've used the Bing search engine, which is AI-powered, to research academic papers, and for fact-checking. I used a spellchecker which is AI-powered. The author examples were found through close reading books with a pencil, and manual search. For pattern search, I began by using the search function and wildcards in Word. Then I developed *Textvizz*, a color-coding text visualization app (see **www.textvizz.com**). My approach will no doubt evolve over time.

I have used AI for learning new skills (how to use a multimeter for electronics, of all things!). I also use it to get context for topics I'm interested in, and to suggest core reading for digging deeper. I find it exceptionally valuable as a friendly general educator, though I wouldn't use it for specifics.

Research suggests that we learn best when we can fit new learning into our existing framework. Think of making a jigsaw puzzle. Typically, you might make the frame first, as it has clear edges which make them easy to join, and gives you a structure.

Meanwhile, you have a pile of free-floating pieces. You might spot patterns or colours that suggest a connection. You'll start grouping them together, joining things up where you can. Bigger and bigger pieces can be joined together – until you only have a few stray pieces to slot into place, with great satisfaction! Which, as an aside, may be due to the Zeigarnik effect – the brain's feeling of closure when outstanding items are "sorted" and disappear from our brain's working memory, which can only hold around seven items at once.

Quite a digression! But it illustrates the point that fitting new learning into our existing context is highly effective and productive. ChatGPT is great at explaining complex concepts in layman terms, and you can even ask it for metaphors if you're struggling.

Here's an example explaining the concept of "iteration" when it comes to writing and editing. In the world of publishing, you might use the term "editing pass".

Q: Can you give an example of a useful metaphor to explain 'iteration' when it comes to writing and editing?

ChatGPT: Sure! Here's a useful metaphor to explain 'iteration' in the context of writing and editing:

Metaphor: Sculpting a Statue from Marble

Initial Block of Marble: *Imagine you start with a rough block of marble. This block represents your first draft. It's unrefined and bulky, just like an initial draft of your writing, which might be filled with rough ideas and unpolished sentences.*

First Chiseling: *The first time you start chiseling away at the marble, you begin to shape it into a rough outline* *of what you envision. In writing, this is your first round of edits where you start refining the structure, correcting obvious errors, and shaping your ideas.*

Further Refinements: *With each subsequent chiseling session, you add more detail and remove more unnecessary material. Similarly, with each iteration of editing your writing, you refine your ideas, improve the clarity, and enhance the flow. You may also cut out parts that don't fit well or add new details that enhance the overall piece.*

Final Polishing: *The final stages of sculpting involve polishing the marble to smooth out any remaining roughness and bring out the fine details. In writing, this is your final round of edits and proofreading, where you perfect your word choices, ensure grammatical accuracy, and make your prose shine.*

Finished Statue: *Eventually, the block of marble is transformed into a beautiful, detailed statue. Through iterative writing and editing, your initial rough draft is transformed into a polished, coherent, and compelling piece of writing.*

Conclusion: *Just as a sculptor iterates through many stages of chiseling and polishing to create a masterpiece from a rough block of marble, a writer iterates through multiple drafts and edits to produce a well-crafted piece of writing.*[98]

The writing itself is rather generic – as you might expect from an AI – and it's not in my voice. But the conceptual "thinking" is useful. If you're struggling to clarify your thoughts and need a sounding board, you might consider it.

Meanwhile, back to some thoughts about AI in general. How is it different from any other digital writing tool?

The line between what's a helpful writing tool, and what's going too far, is becoming very blurred, especially at a time when AI is already incorporated invisibly into writing apps, and other digital tools have speeded up many areas of the writing process.

We're all learning about this new world as it develops. Your own experiments are just as valid as mine. For what it's worth, here are my thoughts. Note, I haven't taken account of copyright issues over texts used to build language models – this is in flux as the creative and writing unions work together on solutions that will hopefully acknowledge and pay creators.

Firstly, AI undoubtedly produces generic, bland text and summaries very well. However, these basic writing genres have limited interest if you're a creative writer. Readers want to hear your vivid, distinctive voice and stories, feel a human connection and emotions, and enjoy immersing themselves in your characters and worlds. And why would you pass on the joyous, creative, unique part of writing to a machine?

Secondly, I feel that bypassing the work of writing isn't just lazy, it's also problematic.

If we outsource writing to an exobrain, not only do we then produce homogenized text, like mixing paint colours to produce a serviceable but dull sort of brown. We also lose the ability to do it ourselves.

If we're not practising writing, we're not learning it. As you know, learning takes place in the stretch zone of human learning. Not stretching your brain's ability means not learning something new.

Deliberate practice can help, by putting focus not just on word production – which can now be done at alarming speed with next to no effort. Rather, you're learning how writing works, how it creates its effects, how to shape it for impact.

If no one studies writing, the reasons for writing in certain ways, the rhetorical, emotional and psychological effects, how words are received, are in danger of being lost. And that makes us vulnerable.

Delegating writing without understanding what it can do makes communication an empty and sometimes powerfully dangerous gesture, as we can see from the torrents of online political propaganda disguised as social interaction.

169

Maybe the most valuable part of writing will become the "how", the learning, and understanding what words – fake words, human words, fake stories, human stories – can do to us. Their means and mechanisms, many of them centuries old, which are used across languages and cultures. Maybe learning about the power of words can help to protect us, as well as giving us a better understanding of a wonderfully expressive creative medium?

Part 7

Writing Visualization

"PICTURES ARE NOT INCIDENTAL
FRILLS – THEY ARE ESSENTIAL TO
THE MIND'S WORK"
– OLIVER SACKS

Words and visualization have a very long history together. To a visiting alien, written English looks like a subtle code that needs to be deciphered – and it is! Mostly, we're so used to reading that we take it for granted.

But our present alphabet actually evolved from pictures – things from everyday life in ancient times. *A hand, a door, an ox, a bird, an eye.*

Our familiar English alphabet traces back to Egyptian hieroglyphs – an ancient writing system based on symbols which represented objects, animals, and ideas. For example, the letter "A" is thought to represent an ox's head.

Hieroglyph　Proto-Sinaitic　Phoenician　Paleo-Hebrew

The ox-head pictogram evolved into the Phoenician *aleph*, was absorbed into Greek as *alpha¸* then into the Roman alphabet we use today.

I find it fascinating to see the modern Greek alphabet and its letters α for alpha and others still showing signs of their pictorial origins: Κ (*kappa*) representing the fingers of the hand; Τ (*tau*) representing a mark or cross; Λ (*delta*) representing a door.

And today, we've come full circle with the emergence of emoticons – modern-day pictograms.

Like words and letters, they mean different things to different people. And they even have different fonts! I used the "dancing lady" emoticon for years till I saw what a friend was seeing at his end – a marching boy. My intention was to send creative enthusiasm, and he was receiving what looked like a young paramilitary.

Words aren't that different, really. The same word can be transmitted and received with entirely different meanings, even without a language difference.

Take the word *close*, for example. It can be received as "shut", "nearby", or – if you're Scottish – a narrow alleyway.

And it can have subtext or irony. Depending on how you say it, "*close*" can mean "*close, but no cigar*" – so, a narrow fail. "*We're close*" can mean everything from having a big loving family to a hint at a secret affair.

Most of us are used to understanding irony, hints and hidden meanings. And the open nature of words is very familiar to actors, playwrights, and comedians.

But few of us – even writers – think deeply about that shapeshifting quality, that shimmering fragility that hits our eyes and ears.

Try thinking of words as a kind of bubble. They look clear and well-defined, but are actually quite fragile. The spoken word, for example, is often tentative, and evolves and takes shape as we speak. The written word may be more highly edited and seem more authoritative when it's in a book or poster or letter – but is it really? And what about the text we write ever day, in emails, text messages, sticky notes – swift tiny utterances from our clumsy fingers and distracted brains?

It's good to appreciate words as a fascinating shimmering current of human life, but also to bear in mind that they don't always deserve our awe, respect, or even attention.

Sometimes, words are just passing thoughts in transmissible form. If you've ever tried mindful meditation, you'll be familiar with the idea of thoughts as bubbles that you don't control.

I find this exceptionally helpful as a writer – for forgiving and appreciating the wildest excesses of my fevered brain (which we all have), and also for practising healthy informality towards a skill we've mostly learned at school, in a formal setting.

That, and the typical writers' veneration for authors they admire, can set us up to feel slightly in awe of words, and may be a contributor to writer's block.

And that's just considering word *transmission*, not *receiving*.

When we consider that anyone reading or listening to us comes with their own language, baggage, projections, mindset, focus, abilities, social context, affinities… it's a wonder we're understood at all!

With so much conflict in the world, it's a wonder more time isn't spent on understanding these dynamics, and their effect on our lives. And the effect of so many English native speakers who may not need to learn other languages, ever.

This might feel like a digression, but for a writer, it's extremely useful. With our words, we're trying to meet people halfway – the place where our intention and their reception intersect.

Try imagining the word-bubbles as a Venn diagram with overlapping circles. The overlap is our shared universal human experience.

Your dog isn't the same as my dog. Your sun isn't the same as mine. Your family isn't the same as mine. But we connect through shared experiences with *dog, sun, family*.

Words are a symbol that connects us with shared ideas. Through the page or screen, you're sending a tiny bolt of lightning from mind to mind. It will resonate in very different ways, but there's a shared essence.

Words act like tiny metaphors, which are open in meaning, yet trigger specific memories and understandings in people who receive them.

They can also direct and misdirect our thoughts. Think about the word *roadkill* for a moment. Is it really *roadkill*? Or is it *carkill*? Or *driverkill*?

Words are both crude and precise; shallow, fleeting bubbles, and profound, powerful tools.

They can never fully capture our experience, but they can evoke, suggest and direct, activating the shared pictures and memories in our readers' minds.

Why is this important for writers? Because of the connection between *symbols* and *meaning*.

Writing is a visual representation of meaning, in a compact way, through symbols. These symbols can represent things, numbers, ideas.

In writing, symbols are combined to form patterns – extraordinary and complex patterns which allow us to convey rich, complex meanings.

Writing has structures and patterns that can be hard to spot, unless you highlight them in some way – say, with visuals.

Visualization can be as simple as using a big headline font to show the main theme of the writing.

Or underlining, bold or italics to emphasize different words.

Or the use of new lines or asterisks, to introduce a new paragraph, section or chapter.

Or colours to emphasize sections we want to return to when we're editing.

We're so used to doing this in our main language that we take it for granted. But imagine you're faced with a big stone tablet carved with Egyptian hieroglyphs. What patterns would you spot then?

You might see that some hieroglyphs are grouped inside a border, and draw special attention. These groups repeat here and there. Could they be names? Names of important people?

That's how scholars deciphered the Rosetta Stone. The repeat patterns of *square, bread, lasso, lion, owl* … represented the sounds *P, T, O, L, M* – and the name *Ptolemy*, a Greek pharaoh.

And this border – called a *cartouche* – works in a similar way to bold, caps or underlining. It's a visual way to draw attention, amid the mass of symbols.

Now, if you're a writer, and language is made up of patterns, what other patterns can be visualized, so you can see what's going on amid the mass of letters?

Let's look at some writing visualization tools – manual and digital – and an introduction to my text visualizer, *Textvizz*.

Visualization – Manual

When I started close reading favourite authors to learn from their techniques, I used a pencil to make notes. This was a big leap for a book lover who was precious about books, especially when I was a student.

Gradually, I became less precious, and now happily use pens and different coloured markers. And those early pencilled student books have themselves become treasures which show what I was thinking about at the time. Mostly, I was just learning new words. These days, I'm learning writing techniques. Your own deliberate practice will depend not just on your interests, but also on the stage you're at.

The idea of marking up books might be alarming if you love physical books as objects. If they're special treasures, you might want to get a cheap second-hand copy just for defacing. I sometimes do this.

Over time, I developed ways to annotate features I was interested in – time structures, dramatic techniques, modal verbs, viewpoint. I discovered narratology – the study of how stories are told.

This called for working with bigger chunks of writing – paragraphs, scenes, chapters – which made highlighters and pens impractical.

Instead, I used cut-ups and sticky notes, and laid out pages of writing on the floor. I used this to look at scenes from a helicopter height, clarify timelines, see where storylines had got lost or were under- or overwritten.

You'll often see this kind of manual visualization used in storylining – TV show writing. You've probably used it before in some way – marker pens or sticky notes highlighting where you want to excise a character, someone's name has changed, you've planted something that needs later payoff.

In the theatre rehearsal room, I first encountered a director and actors writing on scripts and breaking them into beats – a process called "unit-ing". They were looking for shifts in action, emotion, intention, and making discoveries about the underlying structure of the play. There wasn't a right or wrong answer – rather, it was an effective way to uncover currents below the surface code of writing.[99]

If you've heard of "beat sheets" – used to map dialogue in the screen industries – it's a short leap to trying some unit-ing, to see what you can learn for your writing.

TRY THIS

Print out a scene from a favourite script and try "unit-ing" – mark it up, to break it into beats. Look for moments of change between the characters, moments of dynamic or emotional shift. It might be an action, a line that is some kind of gesture in words (*threat, invitation, boundary-setting, naming*) – which is also an action – or a moment where something is revealed.

TRY THIS

Choose a favourite scene. Imagine a baton of power passing between the characters. Read their lines aloud and mark up where the baton passes. What does this reveal about the power and status relationship between the characters? Does it change in the course of the scene? Can you draw this as a shape?

TRY THIS

Write your own scene, using the shape you've discovered. Set it somewhere far away from the original scene, in a different era, with very different characters. This is a draft. Now change the dynamics of the scene to make it your own. What happens if you disrupt expectations, switch the status or baton of power, introduce a new character? Can you draw the new shape?

Big structure – timelines and maps

Your writing will feel more grounded and realistic if you convey a clear handle on time and place. Visual tools can help you to think this through.

Some writers use corkboards or whiteboards to plan their story and plot timeline. Again, these are visual ways to step back from words and see the bigger picture.

I've sometimes used a roll of wallpaper on the floor to explore backstory. You can literally look down on your story world and see the sweep of story, with an almost godlike view.

Wallpaper rolls are also useful for working with actors and clarifying character backstory. If they were born in 1922, how old were they and what were they doing in 1930? In 2000?

What age were their parents at the same time? What was going on in the historial background?

Note, this isn't just about fact-checking and consistency. It's also about depth and a sense of realism.

As a writer deep in the flow of words, you may not have thought through your characters in much detail.

You know what they burningly want, you know what's stopping them, and you have a strong sense of their voice and powers. But you may not know the richness, intricacy and colour of their everyday existence as people.

179

That's fine. Many writers work this way – they know the bare bones, and discover the detail as they go along.

Timelines are a good tool for discovering backstory and fleshing out the detail which really brings characters to life.

But rather than trying to build a whole epic, detailed backstory for all your characters, which could easily become overwhelming, try creating snapshots on the timeline – tiny moments in full sensory depth, rather than all the facts of a lifetime.

There's a useful lesson for writers in the Sandra Bullock comedy, *The Proposal*.[100] Bullock plays an impossible publishing boss who's about to get deported, and seizes on her hapless assistant for a marriage of convenience. They have to get to know each other enough to convince the deportation authorities.

It's a familiar film trope, but what struck me was they started sharing not just factual information, favourite foods, colours, places and people – which you'd naturally expect – but also ordinary moments, memories and disagreements.

What kinds of details create the intimacy that comes from deep shared knowledge over many years?

How can you use snapshots to deepen your character timeline, without spending a lifetime on research?

TRY THIS

Use a roll of paper to plot your character's life, from birth and right through your storyline. Pick a key moment in your character's early life and describe it in detail. What was going on around them? Who was with them? Use all your senses to create an immersive picture of them in their lives. What do you most care about? Pick another time in their teenage years, and paint another picture. Read out your portraits aloud to someone. What do they notice, relate to, and care about? How might these moments from your character's life resonate with their actions later in life?

Scene structure – props and models

I sometimes use physical objects to represent characters in a scene: fruit, office stationery – whatever is to hand. You could use toys, buttons or coins. The objects become stand-ins for the characters, so you can explore their power dynamics and key moments in the story.

Playing with objects is also a good way to get a helicopter view, away from the mental and visual clutter of words.

It also provides a tactile way to explore spatial relationships, which reflect the power, status and needs between characters.

This is also a visual way to think about dramatic techniques, and what you're showing through action, rather than reflection.

Why does this work? Because a physical representation makes the abstract tangible. The essence of relationships is much easier to see.

You can then experiment with the dynamics of space and character actions, and clarify your scene.

TRY THIS:

Choose a few small objects to represent your characters. Set them up for the start of your scene. Now move them around, to see different kinds of interaction. Experiment with *close/far*, *high/low*, *hidden/in the open*, *public/private*, *holding secrets* or *significant objects*.

Now, use props to change the setting. What happens to the scene if one character is behind a door, in a vehicle, on a platform? Can you create a *from/to* visualization that crystallizes a key moment in the action of the scene? See how small changes affect the flow and tension between characters.

Visualization – Digital

The digital era has given writers so many ways to visualize their writing and make it easier to "see" patterns and structures at different scales.

Some of these are dedicated writer tools, but you don't need to go there. You can improvize super-useful tools from software you already have.

Here are some of my favourite visual tools from Microsoft Office 365 Word. Other word processing apps have similar features.

Helicopter view

In the bottom right corner of your Word document, there's a Zoom slider. This lets you shrink your work in progress to a tiny size, giving you an overview of all the pages. (You may need to click *View>Print Layout* in the top navigation.)

I love this view, as I can see my work in progress grow, and get a tangible sense of pages already written, and still to write.

This view is also helpful for showing highlights. For example, I use yellow highlights to show issues still to be solved, blue for quotes to be checked, and a pink marker when doing an editing or proofing pass, so I don't lose my place.

When your book is almost finished, this view is also a great way to spot layout issues, such as changes in font size, or inconsistent margins. Anything inconsistent stands out, so you can spot it and zoom in to check.

Colours are an extra powerful way to make writing notes and features stand out.

Editorial process

If you're working with a remote editor, colours and visualizations are a great way to speed up your process.

In Word, I use the *Comments* feature to insert a note on issues I want to revisit later. It's essentially a placeholder or tag that lets you quickly add a note, without disturbing the flow of writing.

To do this, either click *Insert>Comment* from the top level navigation, or use the keyboard shortcut *CTRL+M (Mac symbol+M)*.

When it comes to an editing pass, you can then make all comments visible by clicking *Review>Show Comments*, and click through and handle them one by one.

This is a huge timesaver if you're working on a longform project.

If you ever receive an edited manuscript full of changes and want to reduce the clutter or switch them off, click *Review>All Markup* and use the dropdown options.

Using Styles with colours

If you're writing alternating character viewpoints, or want to get a handle on wavering viewpoint, try using Styles with colour coding.

Styles have so many uses. They can help you to see how much airtime is given to your characters throughout your novel.

You can then view it using the Zoom slider, and make sure your main character isn't upstaged by a secondary character.

Or, you can use it to highlight dialogue sections, to get a sense of the balance between dialogue, action and description.

To highlight large sections of text, you can use the mouse to drag and select.

I find the mouse really hard on the hands, and always use keyboard shortcuts. Click twice to select a paragraph, then highlight using the icon that appears.

Clicking to colour-code is fine for small chunks of writing, but has its limits if you want to use it a lot. I also find the highlight colours in Word limited and unsubtle, so I use the versatile Styles technique.

With Styles, you can apply a set of style features wherever that Style appears, throughout your entire document. Say you want to change all the headlines to a bigger font – simply change the Style, not each individual headline. With Styles, it's as if each kind of paragraph has its own branding guidelines. Change the branding guidelines, and all those paragraphs get the same style makeover.

Styles are an extremely powerful feature, and widely used in professional book design tools such as Adobe InDesign.

Here's the low-cost way to get the same features, using Word.

TRY THIS

If Styles are new to you, paste some text into a new document (don't use work in progress!), click *Home* and open the *Styles* box. Enlarge its size by dragging the edges of the box, so you can see the dropdown of available styles. Play around with your text by clicking on different styles. You can always revert by clicking *CTRL+Z (Mac symbol+Z)*.

TRY THIS

These Styles are all connected to the specific Word template you're in. There are lots more to play with! Click *Design* at the top of your window, and you'll see a range of templates. Once you can make your own Styles – coming up next – you can also make your own templates – a great way to make sure your manuscripts look consistent and polished for sending out.

TRY THIS

Modify a Style. This is the key to setting up colour coding for paragraphs. To do this, click a Style for your current paragraph – try *Style Intense Quote*, or *Heading 2*. This will clearly change it from *Normal* or *BodyText*, your default style, making sure you don't inadvertently change your entire document. Now, in the Style box, right-click on *Style* (the active Style should have a box round it – scroll down if it's not visible). Click the *Modify* option to open the parameters to change the Style. This is a superpowerful feature where you can change all sorts of parameters but for now, look for *Formatting>Automatic* – a dropdown menu – change the colour, and click *OK*. Remember, you can instantly undo by clicking *CTRL+Z (Mac symbol+Z)*.

TRY THIS

Save a new Style. To save the new coloured Style you've just created, right-click and open the *Modify* window. Change the name at the top and click *Add to the Styles gallery* below. Make sure *Automatically update* and *New documents based on this template* are ticked. This will make your new Style available to other documents you create. Name your Style in a way that's useful and memorable for you. I sometimes add a project name or my initials, so it's clear it's my Style – *JHheader1*. Click *OK*. Now, to use your new Style, simply click its name in the Style box.

TRY THIS

Now you've got the principle, you have a powerful visual tool. Once you allocate a Style – say, *MyNewStyle* – to a paragraph, you can change the appearance of all *MyNewStyle* paragraphs globally. You don't need to do it individually, by hand. It's as though each paragraph type has its own branding guidelines. You just change the branding guidelines, and all the *MyNewStyle* paragraphs get a style makeover.

You can use Styles to create, for example, *RomeoPOVStyle* and *JulietPOVStyle* in different colours, for a novel using alternating character viewpoints. Or to highlight character dialogue.

If you're concerned about overusing flashback, reflection or dream sequences, or have a tendency to go off on a tangent, you could use Styles to highlight these sections, and check the balance between present action, and other sections. You could even make Styles for *show* and *tell*.

Note, this isn't about creating a wildly colour-coded book – though you can go that route if you like! It's simply an editing tool to help you see patterns, assess what's going on, and spot potential problems.

Maybe Romeo is getting far more airtime than Juliet?

Maybe there's too much flashback, and it's holding up present action?

One final advantage of using Styles is that if you self-publish, they reduce errors in book layout. Your books will look more polished, and it's easy to make tweaks globally.

Other visual parameters in Styles can be accessed from the *Styles* box, *Modify, Format* dropdown.

This is extremely powerful and too detailed to go into here – if you're interested, play around with it.

I often use *Format>Font* (for font size and type), *Format>Paragraph* (for indents, margins and line spacing), *Format>Border* (for background shading – another kind of colour visualization).

Professional software tools

Professional writing software tools such as *Scrivener* and *Final Draft* make good use of colour coding for scenes, character presence, actions, and effects.

Final Draft has a useful function where you can print out a breakdown of how many lines each character has, and the lines spoken by a single character. In a film script, this is a great way to check whether a character is underwritten, or whether your main character's lines give enough exciting opportunities for the star – or whether the supporting cast is likely to upstage them.

Although these are fantastic apps – and Final Draft is essential for professional scriptwriters – I sometimes find that the huge number of features get in the way of writing. Many creative editing features can be replicated in Word.

Introducing *Textvizz*

I'm a writer-teacher, and taught creative writing with The Open University in the UK for many years, at undergraduate level, and also on the postgraduate MA course. But I began to get frustrated.

In this section, I'll explain why, and what I went on to do about it: *Textvizz* – a text visualization app that highlights different aspects of language, for more effective teaching.

OU students are wonderful – highly motivated adult learners from all backgrounds and walks of life, with interesting stories to tell. Often, they don't realise how great their material is, because it's familiar to them, and they take it for granted. In a world of publishing which is still skewed towards certain kinds of people and social classes, their stories are a breath of fresh air.

But there's only so much time, there was a huge amount to learn and read, and by the time the students really got going, the course was over.

I wanted a quicker, more systematic way to teach writing craft foundations, to give writers some solid practical techniques. With this overview, they could then concentrate fully on developing what was unique to them – their stories, voice, viewpoint, process.

With a background in languages and music learning, I was particularly keen to share practical language techniques and deliberate practice. I'd found them transformative for my own writing.

I'd often wondered: What if you could *show* this? Rather than explain or tell. *Show* versus *tell*? Now there's a thought!

One of my students was having problems with viewpoint and head-hopping – jumping in and out of different character heads. This created a sense of dislocation, and made the story hard to follow.

But he couldn't see exactly where the jumps were happening in the text – after all, you're just looking at a mass of words. How do you spot the jumps?

I realised that the problem could be seen in the language. By highlighting aspects of the text, I could help to show the linguistic markers of head-hopping.

These were things like consistent pronouns, attribution and verbs of perception. If they were done well, the storytelling was anchored in the main character viewpoint.

The student could now see what to do. They were small, straightforward edits, but they made a huge difference.

Another time, I was working with a client on their new website content. The old content was too corporate-sounding, and customers weren't engaging.

Again, this problem could be seen in the language: use of pronouns, abstract nouns and jargon.

I could of course explain this to the client, but how to *show* it, amid the mass of words?

By visualizing aspects of the text – this time, with a word cloud – I was able to show what was going on, and more importantly, what could be improved.

This helped to make the case for transforming the website content. The difference could be felt by readers, and shown to management.

By now, I was sure I was onto something. But something was missing: a tool to make it easy to show these differences.

Fast-forward a couple of years, with the help of grant and a gifted developer, I created the tool I wanted: *Textvizz*.

Textvizz is a text visualizer that highlights different features of the English language, making teaching, learning and showing much easier.

It can be used for all levels of writing craft, from beginner basics to advanced stylistics, and it's a great tool for deliberate practice and study. Currently, I'm using it for writing courses and teaching.

If you're interested in *Textvizz* and visual writing training, please join my mailing list: **www.textvizz.com**.

You can also contact me direct through **info@method-writing.com**, and find out more about my teaching background at **www.method-writing.com**.

The same face: the very same. Marley in his pigtail, usual waistcoat, tights and boots; the tassels on the latter bristling, like his pigtail, and his coat-skirts, and the hair upon his head. The chain he drew was clasped about his middle. It was long, and wound about him like a tail; and it was made (for Scrooge observed it closely) of cash-boxes, keys, padlocks, ledgers, deeds, and heavy purses wrought in steel. His body was transparent; so that Scrooge, observing him, and looking through his waistcoat, could see the two buttons on his coat behind.

Noun vizz showing the corporeal appearance of Marley's ghost in Dickens' *A Christmas Carol*.

— I love living here. It's a different universe. The house is just wow — early Victorian, a 'terrace' - unassuming- looking outside but massive inside — but there's still a kind of humility that really appeals to me - almost everything white, and a lot of handmade things, and quilts and dark wood shelves and cornices and this four-storey staircase - and in the whole place there's only one television, which is in the basement anyway, just so Monty can keep abreast of news stuff, and some of the things he does on the television - but that's it. I think of it as the

Visualization of conjunctions *and/but* showing flow of sentence in Zadie Smith's *On Beauty*.

living this was the first morning of summer
Douglas Spaulding, twelve, freshly wakened, let
summer idle him on its early-morning stream.
Lying in his third-story cupola bedroom, he felt
the tall power it gave him, riding high in the
June wind, the grandest tower in town the trees
washed At night, when together, he flashed his
gaze like a beacon from this lighthouse in all
directions over swarming seas of elm and oak
and maple. Now .. Boy,' whispered Douglas A
whole summer ahead to cross off the calendar,
day by day. Like the goddess Siva in the travel
books, he saw his hands jump everywhere,
pluck sour apples peaches, and midnight
plums. He would be clothed in trees and
bushes and rivers. He would freeze, gladly, in
the hoar- frosted ice house door. He would bake
happily, with ten thousand chickens, in

See how Ray Bradbury's verbs animate the landscape, and
modals situate Douglas's wistful vision in *Dandelion Wine*.

'Josie will be so happy when she hears.' 'Maybe
tomorrow even.' 'Yes, of course. Well then,
goodbye. It was a very interesting trip for me.
Thank you for your useful advice.' 'See you,
Klara. Go carefully.' The timing of my journey to
Mr McBain's barn, as I'd told Rick, was crucial,
and when I crossed the loose stones towards
the picture frame gate for the second time that
dayFHAM, a fear came into my mind that I'd
miscalculated. The Sun was already low before
me — and I couldn't assume the second and
third fields would be as easy to navigate as the
first. noises around me, making me fearful that
I'd made a serious miscalculation, that there
was no justifiable reason to disturb his privacy
in the manner I was hoping to do, that my

See Kazuo Ishiguro's use of adjectives to depict his unusual
viewpoint character in *Klara and the Sun*. What can we
learn about her?

Part 8

The Science of Excellence

There's a whole world of research into excellence, undertaken by psychologists and educators who want to understand how the learning brain works, and help people to learn more effectively. The word "mastery" has come under scrutiny for its associations with dominance and control, but it's worth a look at its early origins. "Master" and the related word "maestro" are derived from *magister*, the Latin word for teacher, or expert.

Within mediaeval trade guilds, the master was a leader responsible for teaching apprentices. In those days, you'd come through the apprentice scheme yourself, learn your craft, and gradually rise in the hierarchy, to the point where you'd pass your skills on. You're someone who has earned their chops, and a certain status, within your profession.

The following summaries bring together the main research findings from several of these magisters, together with suggestions on how you might apply them to your writing.

Peak: Secrets from the New Science of Expertise
Professor Anders Ericsson and Robert Pool[101]

Anders Ericsson was a cognitive psychologist and expert on the science of expertise. His research on deliberate practice and performance has had a major influence on our understanding of skills acquisition and mastery. He also inspired Gladwell's *Outliers*.

Peak focuses on deliberate practice as a route to excellence, and questions the importance of innate talent. His research case studies focus on musicians, athletes, and chess players. Ericsson also discusses the workings of our brains when it comes to learning skills. When we practise something repeatedly, this strengthens our neural pathways, through a process called *myelination*. This means that through practice, a protective coating (*myelin*) is formed around our nerve fibres, which helps to increase the effectiveness of electrical signal transmission in your brain. So deliberate practice is making changes in a very specific, physical way, deep inside our brains!

Practical applications for writers

Ericsson's work on deliberate practice is discussed earlier in this book, along with a breakdown of its main elements: focused, structured practice, specific goals, and feedback. There are lots of examples of deliberate practice patterns to try. Once you've done this, take the next step of creating your own patterns to explore writing questions you're interested in.

Peak goes on to discuss another component of expertise: mental representations. Ericsson's examples from the world of chess are particularly interesting here, as chess, like writing, is a less physical activity than music-making or sport. Players use mental pictures to visualize their moves several steps in advance, and need to think at different structural scales, and in different dimensions, balancing many elements at once. This multi-tasking, multi-stranded thinking is familiar from writing. Chess also has a sense of narrative shape, with two sides in battle against each other – not unlike the tensions between protagonist and antagonist in storytelling.

For writers, visualizations can be a great help, especially for structuring long-form writing. Even if you're not mainly a visual thinker, looking at your writing at a remove from word and sentence level can help you to think more objectively about its shapes and patterns. There are two main areas where this can be useful: shaping your story, and improving your process.

I often use sketches, colours, timelines and storyboards in my writing. These are more than mental representations – I see them as essential workings for keeping a handle on storylines which would otherwise bifurcate endlessly, like overgrown bushes. Cinema-style storyboarding and "shot" thinking (wide shot, close-up, etc) is great for framing your writing viewpoint, and helps with editing. Colours are good for different character plotlines. I've often used wallpaper rolls to map out timelines – both for my plot, and for character and event timelines.

Some of these visualizations are provided in professional writing software, such as Scrivener, used mainly by prose writers, or Final Draft, used by screenwriters. I've tried both, and find they create a bit of a barrier to the flow of writing. But lots of professional writers swear by them, and I suspect I just haven't spent the time getting used to them.

Meanwhile, you can do a lot of useful visualizations just with Microsoft Word. Try *View>Outline* for a helicopter view of your book chapters and sections. Click through the different levels to see chapter headings and rearrange sections, without the distraction of paragraph detail. Use *View>Styles* to set up colour-coded paragraph Styles for draft, edit, and proof stages. With the Zoom slider in the bottom right of your screen, zoom out to display your entire book in a single window. If you use colours to mark up placeholders for research, or further editing, you can see these outstanding jobs at a glance. It's also satisfying to see your book grow as you write.

Colour can now also be used to visualize words in new ways, thanks to digital tools capable of handling large amounts of data. My writing app, *Textvizz*, colour-codes parts of speech, such as verbs, nouns and adverbs, so you can take a closer look at style and variety in your writing. It's also a great tool for studying stylistics – the style features of authors in general. You can also do this with a highlighter pen.

Pushing beyond your comfort zone is another key aspect of the findings in *Peak*. As discussed, by design, deliberate practice is aimed at the slightly uncomfortable edge of your comfort zone, at the point of *eustress*. But what about other ways of extending your comfort zone? Here are some ideas:

Experiment with reading in genres you don't normally consider. Maybe science fiction, fantasy, romance, or political speeches? Then try writing in that genre.

Take part in a writing conference. It's a chance to hear inspiring speakers, meet other writers, and get fired up by shared enthusiasm. And if you want to really smash your comfort zone, offer yourself as a speaker.

Collaborate with another writer. If possible, write a piece together. Or share an experience together, write about it, and edit each other's work. What can you learn from each other's strengths and weaknesses? Could you complement each other in a bigger collaboration? With remote technology, you can even try writing in the same document at the same time. Screenwriters sometimes work as a team, editing, drafting and discussing together, while seeing their script take shape on the screen. If you're a control freak, this will be incredibly hard! But it also replicates the give-and-take you need when working closely with an editor, so it's interesting to try.

Go on a writing date. Not a romantic moment with a neighbourhood novelist, but a date with yourself. Go somewhere you haven't been before, treat yourself to a new taste or experience, walk a new route, discover a new view. New experiences are refreshing, and help to shake up your brain, and make new neural connections. If you're struggling with your writing at any point, this can also be a good way to practise self-care.

Set writing challenges. In the online world, people often do challenges such as the 100-day challenge, or the daily photograph. How might you adapt this to your writing? I once committed to 100 days of writing microfiction. Each took five minutes, was based on a random prompt from a random book, and the stories were published as a short fiction collection, *Nanonovels*.[102]

Another approach is the **48-hour film challenge**, which has become its own festival. Participants go from initial prompt to a complete short film for screening, in just two days. If that's all the time you have, what's essential? What do you leave out? What clever shortcuts do you find? How do you keep on track? The writing equivalent might be to write a short story in a day, or a poem a day, for a month. Think about accountability, too – are you going to post it online, or send it out to a magazine? Challenges like this can help you to tackle perfectionism and fears about rejection head-on.

Commit to competitions. Even if competitions aren't your thing, they can be a good way to stretch your comfort zone, by giving you a non-negotiable deadline, and usually a word count to write to. Again, accountability can help you to stick to your commitment. Tell people what you're doing. Or take on the challenge along with a writing buddy.

Creative constraints. Write some rules for yourself, put them in a hat, and pick one out at random. Try *just one page, 100 words, rhyming couplets, no vowel "e", child viewpoint, inanimate object viewpoint, concrete poem, sonnet, acrostic*. Although these are exercises, they can lead you in a productive direction. French author Georges Perec famously wrote an entire novel without the letter "e", *La Disparition*, translated by Gilbert Adair into English as *A Void*. Flash fiction can be turned into a collection, or printed on postcards.

Body double. This online phenomenon emerged during the pandemic, as a way for homeworkers to replace the company and accountability of coworkers. It has evolved into remote coworking, often by small peer groups who don't often get to see each other face to face. If you're used to writing on your own, this will be a stretch! An alternative I've used is a WhatsApp group of writers who cheer each other on doing writing sprints.

Tiny Habits
Professor B.J. Fogg[103]

B.J. Fogg is a pioneering behavioural scientist, and founder of the Behavior Design Lab at Stanford University. His bestseller *Tiny Habits* is a refreshing antidote to the idea that you can only making lasting changes in your life by applying grit and willpower. His approach, based on 20 years of research and experience coaching many thousands of people, advocates small, easy-to-do actions which build into habits over time.

Fogg introduces a number of science-based strategies to make change easier. They include:

Start small to achieve big

"Tiny" really does mean tiny! Above, I've mentioned the idea of "laughably simple" goals, such as a five-minute writing stint. Fogg's findings suggest that by setting the bar low and manageable, you remove excuses and the effect of resistance. Once you've started, you've overcome that invisible threshold, and it's far easier to build momentum. I can testify to using this successfully in several areas of life, including exercise and meditation. It links well to the "streak" idea mentioned previously.

Practical applications for writers

Often, we set ourselves unsustainable targets, emulating successful authors we've heard about – 1,000, 2,000, 3,000 words a day, or *NaNoWriMo*, the 50k November writing challenge. But it's so easy to run out of steam, or hit a difficult day, and give up, then feel like a failure. Fogg advocates a "stealth" approach that neatly sidesteps "all-or-nothing" thinking.

Set yourself a target so small and ridiculous that you can't fail to meet it. When I had writers' block after being off ill for a while, I began writing five-minute daily stories, to help with recovery and to meet resistance head-on. Five minutes of writing a day didn't

198

leave me any wiggle room for excuses. I used random prompts taken from books on my bookshelf. The simple commitment forced me to *just start*, and the stories eventually became a book of flash fiction, *Nanonovels*. You can try it for yourself using my *Nanonovels 30-Day Challenge Workbook*.

Tiny habits are a great way to introduce deliberate practice into your life. When do you read? Morning, evening? On your commute to work? Keep a notebook – or use your diary – and note just one inspiring sentence each day. Look at it closely and see what you can learn from it. Choose one aspect – its structure, rhythm, viewpoint, register – and write three practice sentences of your own. Even if you don't have time for morning pages, you still have five minutes to write a *nanonovel* or practice sentences.

Anchor habits to existing routines

You may have heard of this as *habit stacking*. We all have some routines we manage to stick to, even if it's simply to shower or eat breakfast in the morning. Fogg's *cue-action-reward* model suggests building new habits on top of existing ones. Your current established habit then acts as a cue for the new one. The idea is again to reduce friction through a simple action, avoiding the overthinking that creates resistance.

I tested this out with a new habit of putting a glass of water by my bed at night. On waking up, it was the first thing I saw, so I drank it before even getting out of bed. It has now become part of my routine.

Practical applications for writers

How might you anchor writing in an everyday habit? Perhaps you could write first thing, by putting pen and paper on your bedside table? Or do deliberate practice with an inspirational book you're happy to mark up? Keep your notebook in the kitchen, and write while waiting for the kettle to boil (if you're in the UK!)? Establish a cue to describe five people you see on your commute?

Find your own creative way to use cues and routines to anchor a new fledgling habit.

Reward, Celebration

Use positive reinforcement after you've achieved something, however tiny. This helps to reinforce the habit by releasing dopamine into your brain, strengthening the neural pathway for that habit. What kind of positive reinforcement? Anything you like! It can be something tiny – a smile, a cheer – or a pat on the back or happy dance, if you're feeling enthusiastic. Or gamify your habit by promising a reward after a successful streak or chain.

Practical applications for writers

I admit I'm not great at this one – still a work in progress. But we need to be our own cheerleaders, as we can't expect others to do the job of validating us and our writing. Instead of celebrating major milestones, such as a book publication (easy to love), celebrate your sustained everyday work of showing up at the desk. Focusing on the process of work rather than outcomes means you're appreciating your regular effort and commitment, not just the distant, elusive outcome. Jerry Seinfeld's "Don't Break the Chain" strategy is a good way to do this, if you like external reinforcement. Get a wall calendar and put a big X on it, every day that you write. Or use your diary. Otherwise, make a point of saying "well done". You may be the only person who does! So, you've got to enjoy the process and embrace internal validation.

Outliers: The Story of Success
Malcolm Gladwell[104]

Malcolm Gladwell is a best-selling and highly readable journalist whose books synthesize complex topics in psychology and sociology, making them accessible, and drawing practical conclusions. *Outliers* popularized the psychology research by

Anders Ericsson, establishing the idea that around "10,000 hours" are needed for people to achieve excellence in a given field. Naturally, this is an over-simplification! However, his book does take a close, cool-headed look at the factors beyond individual talent that contribute to success, including deliberate practice, timing, cultural background, and seizing opportunities.

Practical implications for writers

Let's break Gladwell's catchy concept down. 10,000 hours translates into 5½ years of five-day weeks, working seven hours a day. So, doing nothing else, with the weekend and evenings off, you can become an excellent writer – whatever that means!

To give some context, this is roughly the time you'd spend in college education, assuming you also do other things, and have a few holiday breaks. So it's not unrealistic to think of "10,000 hours to mastery" as degree level. It's also roughly the time you might spend as an apprentice in a trade, or in a professional area such as journalism or sales, before being let loose into the world as a master craftsperson, or being put in charge of your own retail branch.

How about the arts? Artists by nature are lifelong learners, always open to discovery, so there isn't the same "you've made it" sense of reaching a panoramic viewpoint where you can now see yourself as an expert. Even a creative writing degree, in my experience, doesn't provide this. Creative writing courses tend to be exploratory and largely self-directed, without the level of granular feedback needed in deliberate practice. Writers rarely emerge from courses as fully-formed publishing-ready professionals. It's far more likely they've explored forms and themes, developed their voice, and produced a substantial draft ready to work up over the next year or so.

If 10,000 hours (or so) are needed to progress from "apprentice" to "master" stage, it makes sense to devote some of them to deliberate practice. Even 15 minutes a day close-reading examples, making notes, will make a difference. Make it part of your morning ritual, commute, or lunch hour. This short exercise will get you thinking as a writer throughout your day.

Opportunities and cultural background

Gladwell doesn't sugarcoat the idea of equal opportunities for all. Some people have special opportunities in their background – the Polgar sisters and their chess-teaching father, for example. Musicians may have access to expensive instruments, sportspeople to kit and equipment, a school with good facilities, and a family passionate about sports. So, anyone aiming to succeed without these advantages will need to try all the harder.

Practical applications for writers

If you have writers in your background, this will certainly help to demystify writing as a job. And you may have an easier route to connections, invitations, and the confidence needed for today's literary life, where you're expected to do your own self-promotion, and have an interesting life story to tell.

If you don't have this background, you're on your own. Yes, doing a creative writing degree course will give you access to publisher or agent introductions. But it's still the writing, storytelling and likely sales that count, and on that score, you're up against everyone else. What's more, degree courses are also typically geared towards literary writing, which is its own niche, with a limited audience. So they may not equip you for the sales- and genre-oriented realities of commercial publishing.

You simply have to write exceptionally well, and have something vital, urgent or wildly appealing to say. Good writing craft is a must.

Gladwell also discusses the "Matthew effect", named after a Bible verse (Matthew 25:29) which suggests "the rich get richer, and the poor get poorer". In terms of success, it points to a kind of "compound interest" – in other words, early advantages lead to increasing advantages over time.

This isn't necessarily bad news. Knowing that the odds are stacked against you can be leveraged to spur you to work harder. It's also well documented that publishing lacks diversity, and white middle class people are over-represented in the arts in general. Your background, voice and viewpoint may well attract publishers interested in fresh stories.

Mindset: The New Psychology of Success Dr Carol Dweck[105]

Carol Dweck is a renowned psychologist and professor at Stanford University, specializing in mindset and its role in success and learning, making her a leading authority in psychology and education.

Dweck's key concept is the difference between *fixed* and *growth* mindsets. With a fixed mindset, people believe their abilities and intelligence can't be changed. This typically leads to them avoiding challenges that would lead to growth. With a growth mindset, on the other hand, you believe your abilities and intelligence can be developed through effort, learning and perseverance. This mindset encourages you to dive into challenges, accept potential failure, and learn from criticism.

Dweck's book includes research on how students with a growth mindset outperform a fixed mindset, and the importance of praise for effort. She also looks at the impact of a growth mindset on athletes and professionals.

Practical applications for writers

Do you have a fixed or growth mindset about writing? Does fear of rejection make you avoid challenges? Or do you tackle a challenge head-on, do your best and learn, or even relish it? If fear of rejection or failure is deep in your mindset, you may avoid sending work out, doing readings and workshops, or even getting started at all.

I know a very well-read, book-loving friend who is so critical that although he often speaks longingly about becoming a writer, he just doesn't write at all. Yet if he accepted the need to start somewhere, embrace the clunky, frustrating, failing side of things, he would learn and progress – just as we all do.

The idea that you don't need to learn, and can magically produce a complete novel through sheer luck and willpower, is responsible for a lot of writer disappointment! It's natural for people to want to protect their egos, and avoid pain. But what if you enjoyed the learning itself, the fun of practising and discovering? And took the pressure off external success you can't control? It could transform your relationship with writing.

The power of *yet*

Changing your language can help you to change your mindset. Watch out for what you tell yourself, and say to others. Dweck suggests that instead of saying "I can't do this", try, "I can't do this *yet*." The tiny word *yet* makes a vital distinction. Rather than closing down all possibility, you're pointing towards future possibility – a glint of hope, and an assertion of personal agency and change. Your timeline opens out with a road to the future, rather than a non-negotiable roadblock.

Similarly, shift your mindset, and see challenges as opportunities for growth. Or, rather than embracing the cliché of "problems = opportunities", embrace the idea of yourself as a problem-solver, with an expert toolkit, and a whole shedload of creativity, ingenuity, and perseverance. Metaphors and language matter. Check in with yourself about language that gets you motivated. What metaphors and language give you energy, and what deplete it? This is highly personal, so you may need to do some digging. If it helps to create a superhero character as your alter ego, do it! You're a writer, after all.

Success of others

Dweck's reframing approach includes rethinking the success of others. It's easy to feel envious, downhearted or threatened when you see others having the success you dream of. But why not get inspired and galvanized instead? Celebrate their success. It hasn't come overnight. They've put in the work. Learn what you can. Above all, realise that you're doing your own thing, with your own drives and skills, while they're doing theirs. There's no point in comparisons. It's like a bird comparing itself with a badger. You're different animals! And you can't do everything, on your limited time on this earth.

Then, decide the next small step, and do it. I find it's easy to get overwhelmed by goalsetting, big plans and milestones, though they work as a general vision. Deadlines do often work if the stakes are very high, but they can equally send me into paralysis. Loving "the sound of deadlines as they woosh by", said by Douglas Adams, the writer of *The Hitchhiker's Guide to the Galaxy*, is likely to make you feel stressed, rather than empowered and positive. But looking closer to home, you *can* do something small in the present. Keeping your action focus doable – even laughably small, such as "open the document" – can work, as it creates momentum.

Early on in my writing adventure, I was in the studio, at the production of my radio script. I'd timed it, but the actors' energetic performance meant that the script was short – about three minutes short, which is a long time for radio dead air. What's more, one of the main actors had to go off to an audition, leaving only the child actor still available. I had to write more material under pressure, in around 15 minutes. The printer wasn't working. The script was handwritten. And the amazing young actor did a beautiful performance that saved the day.

This was a tremendous learning experience. Never again will I go into broadcast production without extra material ready to drop in. It was also rather terrifying. I bunked down in a corner, clamped on earmuffs and got writing. It was my responsibility, and I had to solve the problem for the team. Luckily, I'd done a

205

lot of writing under pressure as a radio journalist, so I was used to the feeling of a clock ticking to the hour, and a story having to be ready to put into the presenter's hands. So I managed not to panic. Looking back, I didn't exactly enjoy it, but was glad to be able to step up, and show resilience under pressure.

Criticism can be a tough one for writers. This can come from several sources: editors, friendly readers, peer group – friendly or hostile – and your own inner critic. Like other success experts, Dweck again suggests using criticism as learning opportunity. But some of it is more important than others. Let's break it down.

The gift of notes

Feedback from editors is a gift. Experts have taken time to read your work, consider it, and give you feedback. In the creative industries, this is often called "notes". I like this term. It feels less top-down than "feedback", and reminds me of professional, collaborative moments in the creative sector.

More on this in a moment.

But first, it's important to recognise that humans are wired to notice the negative more than the positive. You get a wonderful letter full of affirming feedback, and fixate on the two sentences hidden near the end which suggest areas for improvement. Maybe even just two words, which rattle round in your brain for days. Sounds familiar?

If this is you – and let's face it, it's most of us – it's because of the human brain's wiring. Our sensitive amygdala jumps to alert and pumps in chemicals when there's a threat. This is great in evolutionary terms – say, when you're facing a ravenous tiger. But although humans don't face the same dangers today, everyday tiny threats can still fire our brain in the same way.

The problem with this built-in over-sensitivity for writers is that we can take it personally. The combination of the inner work of writing, our vivid internal landscapes, and relatively solitary habits can make our brains a crucible for negative rumination. It's pretty well an occupational hazard.

So with any feedback you receive, remember your brain's exaggeration. Think of those fairground mirrors that twist your body out of shape, or those phone filters that give you monster eyes and alien ears. That's the kind of filter you're seeing through.

So what can you do about it? Imagine you're making a poster for your book. One with stars and reviews blazened across it. Find the positives in your feedback. *Powerful… evocative… intriguing… pacy…* Put them on your imaginary book poster. Or use Canva to make a real one. Keep a "kudos" file of positive feedback – it'll act as an antidote when you're feeling derailed.

Think, too, of the editor who has taken time to focus solely on your work, engaged with it, responded. If you're an early stage writer, considered feedback can take as long as the writing. It's important to value that support, and take it seriously. You don't have to agree with everything. Take whatever you find most helpful, and use it in your deliberate practice.

Remember that editors have read a lot of work in progress. They have a helicopter view of writing issues, and ways to solve them. You're tapping into their knowledge and instincts. You can take them or leave them, of course. But why not learn from their experience?

Imagine sitting down with your production team, just after a performance. The audience have just left the building. The director wants to share some tweaks and practical suggestions, to make tomorrow night's performance really sing. The lighting technician wants to raise a blocking question. The sound technician has a question about volume, now they've had a full house. An actor wants to cut a muddy line, which needs checking with the writer.

The process is brisk, effective, and professional. There's little discussion, and no egos – just cut to the chase, with agreed action steps.

So they have a short list of notes to share. "Turn down the volume on that moment in Act 2." "Give that line more time to land before Antonio's entrance".

Mastery
Robert Greene[106]

Robert Greene is an author and researcher on human behaviour and achievement. While studying the lives of exceptional people such as Leonardo da Vinci, he noticed patterns and similarities in their approach. His best-seller *Mastery* pulls these discoveries together, and offers a framework for making the most of your own skills and passions. Here are some key takeaways, and how you might apply them as a writer.

Discover your calling (Life's Task)

Work out what truly motivates and excites you. This calls for deep introspection.

You only have one life, and limited time. So what truly, deeply motivates you? There's no point in writing genre thrillers to hit a speculative market, if you're far more interested in poetry, or cozy crime.

Firstly, there's no guarantee of financial or any other success, especially in a constantly shifting and unpredictable market. You may not have the skills, the opportunities, or the resilience to push through the difficult times. Your precious time may be wasted on an elusive goal.

It's best to have *intrinsic* goals (inner motivation) than *extrinsic* goals (external motivation) such as money, or even validation from others. You have very little control over external factors, so disappointment is far more likely.

The misalignment will find you out, in the form of boredom, frustration, and an uphill struggle. Pursuing your deep, burning passions, on the other hand, will feel intuitive, exciting, and fulfilling. Even if you don't "succeed" in a conventional sense, you'll still be doing what you love, and finding your place in that world.

Apprenticeship

Greene advises a period of apprenticeship when you learn the foundations of your field. Find mentors, dedicate significant time to practice, and be prepared to fail often, and learn from your failures.

Practical applications for writers

Recognise that you're at beginner stage, and have things to learn – even if you already write in another genre or field. *Mentors* might mean taking courses, joining a writers' group, or reading craft books. I find craft books the fastest way to learn in a focused way, while small groups or a writing buddy are better for accountability. "Dedicating significant time to practice" brings in deliberate practice. *Failing* means getting friendly with rejection, even recognising it as an essential part of writing, to be welcomed as a sign of progress, and growing your skills.

Absorb the hidden knowledge

Greene advocates moving beyond formal knowledge, and getting immersed in the subtleties of a field, including unspoken rules, and learning from others.

Practical applications for writers

Unspoken rules exist in every occupation. In writing, they might include industry secrets, behavioural expectations, the artistic culture, interpersonal politics, financial considerations, or other unexpected factors. Some fields of writing have a hidden expectation that you have a creative writing degree, or an arts background. Others will expect you to have a huge passion for the genre you aspire to write in. Some writers can support their writing from private funds, others can't. Watch out for areas of potential naivety, and only join groups where you can thrive while being yourself. Online writing groups and forums have their own distinct cultures. Watch and learn!

Creative-Active Phase

Greene suggests that after mastering the basics, it's time to innovate, experiment, take risks, and develop your unique style and approach.

Practical applications for writers

It's important to learn from others, and get a good grasp of craft skills. But at some point, you'll move beyond the apprentice stage, and want to make your own mark. Only you can write your books. Your unique combination of voice, world, material and creativity has never existed in the world before. Who knows where that can take you? Maybe further than the writers in your group or course?

So don't be limited by what's around you. Look further, and be open to new ideas and influences. Experiment with new forms, read in different genres, try new kinds of expression. Deliberate practice is a great tool for this, with limitless potential. Read books in translation, speeches, plays, manuals, letters, historical texts – everything helps to shape the writer and thinker you become. You don't need to become an expert in a new field to glean interesting snippets and insights. And you don't need to spend a lot of time, or aim for publishable work. Use deliberate practice as your daily experimental testbed, as a short exercise or *étude*, as a place for risk and stretch well beyond your comfort zone.

Mentorship

Greene stresses the importance of finding the right mentors, and having an evolving, reciprocal relationship.

Practical applications for writers
This is highly individual, and different mentors will be right for different stages. I've mentored several writers, and also received mentoring, though not from another writer. My feeling is that a

210

mentoring relationship is a big ask, and it's best to keep it time-limited, professional, and linked to a clear goal. A loose type of relationship might seem friendlier, but can run out of steam and founder through lack of focus. You don't want to waste the mentor's time, especially if they're exceptionally kind and encouraging, to the point of not setting boundaries for their own work. Expecting a mentor to read sheaves of writing drafts and offer feedback isn't realistic. It's very easy to send file attachments with your week's work, which takes almost as long to read critically as you did to write it. Before you know it, your mentor may have crossed into doing unpaid editorial work under the guise of a friendly mentorship catch-up. Just to reinforce the pitfalls of unstructured mentoring relationships!

My best mentorship experience was in creative product development, where I was learning a tough new skillset, and needed professional guidance. We had monthly check-ins where I asked specific questions, and set specific goals for the next time. My mentor was very busy, we had only six sessions, and I was very motivated to achieve my goals and get the very best from him, and from the experience.

Working with writers' groups and 121, I've found it best to proceed in a similar way, deciding a focus topic each time, agreement about available time, a rough agenda, and some time to check in about targets achieved and for next time. With reading and feedback sessions, we also agree how long to spend. This keeps up a good level of progress, and manageable commitment on both sides.

Social intelligence

Greene mentions social intelligence as a significant element of mastery. Networks are important for finding like-minded people, being alerted to opportunities, and collaborations.

211

Practical applications for writers

The writer equivalent of trade organizations includes professional networks, such as the Society of Authors, the Writers' Guild, and the Alliance of Independent Authors. As well as occasional events, both in person and online, these all have online forums where you can hang out, ask questions, and share advice. One of the challenges here is spending too much fragmented time, and getting distracted from writing. Another is navigating the culture and politics of online forums, which can be hard to tune into. But you can also find out about what's happening in your sector, and make some good friends and contacts in this way.

As an introverted writer who prefers to safeguard precious writing and reading time, I confess this is a hard one for me. But it's possible to network in ways that don't exhaust you. A small group or collective can be more manageable, and you can get together with people with the same kind of aspirations as you. You could also decide on a time-limited programme, to manage expectations about the group continuing in the long term.

It's important to find people who have the same attitude to writing, and love discussing craft, work in progress, sharing plans and projects. With many professional writers, this is off limits. Some writers prefer not to talk about current projects, in case of clumsy comments or unhelpful feedback. For some, the writing process is mysterious, and needs to be protected. Or they may simply be at an advanced stage, far beyond craft discussion with aspiring peers. It can also become tricky when writers apply for the same job opportunities, or you're on a panel for a job your colleague has applied for (or vice versa). These situations crop up in any profession, but it may be a surprise that it happens in a world where people love what they do. You'll need empathy and emotional intelligence to deal with the dark side of success, failure, and creative ups and downs.

Resistance and persistence

Greene makes it clear that the path to mastery is difficult, and resilience and persistence are vital. You'll come up against external and internal obstacles, and need to be able to handle criticism.

Practical applications for writers

More than ever before, writers are exposed to criticism. Reader reviews and online forum comments can cut deep, especially when they have a wide public, and are around for a long time. You need to get, if not exactly comfortable with this reality, at least able to rise above it. One useful tactic is to find something to be grateful about. At least people are reading your work. You're getting an emotional reaction. You've had the guts to raise your head above the parapet enough to be noticed at all. Don't underestimate these achievements.

When it comes to dealing with trolls and unfair comments, it's hard. People have the right to express their opinions about anything at all, and you have no control over that. You only have control of your reaction. Are you going to wade in and feed the trolls? Or be gracious, self-preserve, and use it as fuel for your writing?

Other external factors include time, deadline pressure, and the people around you. You need to manage these, and may have more choices than you think. Resistance can show up in so many disguises, and it's easy to project it onto factors that you can manage to some degree. Look deep, and be really honest about this. What external factors can you mitigate? Can you work in a more productive place, such as a library, café, or hotdesking office? Can you use timeblocks, watch less TV, or get up an hour earlier for writing? Which factors do you have some control over?

In the end, it's always good to remember that it's far more fun than other work people do for a living. The hardship of writing doesn't stack up against the hardship of frontline medicine, law and order, social work, retail, construction work, and so many other jobs.

Again, I find a moment of gratitude helps – I'm doing something I've chosen, and something I love. Any excuses soon evaporate.

It's also important to practise self-care, and be realistic about your energy and resources, and what you can achieve. Just because others are writing a book a month (!), are ever-present in online forums, and popping up on every podcast, doesn't mean that you can. Drive, ambition and will won't take you there, if that's not you. This is a really important recognition, as it's easy to feel guilty or ashamed that you can't work as hard, or as fast, or use other people's process as a yardstick for your success. That way burnout lies.

Recognise that personalities are different, and need different nurturing to thrive. For much of my writing life, I followed role models that were in a different game that didn't suit me at all. I thought I could stare down resistance and work in the same way. Later, after a period of burnout, I did a deep-dive into what made me happy and joyful about writing. It led to becoming much more assertive about my own needs, which was quite a mindset shift.

Becca Symes' books, starting with *Dear Writer, You Need to Quit*[107], are great for a psychology-based approach to working out the processes and nurturing that work best for you. I've discovered a degree of ADHD, and have adapted my writing process to work with it, rather than try to beat it into submission.

I also highly recommend Steven Pressfield's insightful books, *The War of Art*, about resistance and how to conquer it, and its follow-up, *Turning Pro*[108], about the differing habits and mindset of professional versus early-stage writers. They're great companions for each stage of Greene's *Mastery*.

Awakening the Dimensional Mind

At this advanced stage of mastery, rational and intuitive thinking work hand in hand. You're able to draw on wide resources, experiences, and craft skills, and draw on a multi-dimensional approach to problem-solving.

Practical applications for writers

Celebrate! You've studied and practised your craft to a level where you're often tapping into what you know, rather than climbing a mountain with each paragraph. Even if you haven't had a particular problem before, you trust your process, and know you can solve it. Underlying any doubts in your day-to-day writing is a quiet confidence and resilience that can only come from experience.

There isn't an end or plateau to aim for in the writing life. The creative imagination is all about curiosity and discovery, so a place of complacency or self-congratulation won't satisfy you for long. But do take time to appreciate yourself, and your hard-won skills. Don't hide your light under a bushel to make others comfortable. Aspiring writers can learn from you, so be ready to help those who appreciate it. Congratulations on making the journey from apprentice to master!

And finally

Some key points:
* Develop a routine
* Set realistic goals
* Seek feedback
* Stay curious

Practical applications for writers

These elements of the writing process aren't "set and forget". You'll constantly cycle through them, starting new routines, setting new stretch goals, getting more incisive professional feedback, making new discoveries. Writing is an iterative path – think of it as an upward spiral where you return to the same place, from a different vantage point. What's changed in between is your learning and experience. Greene's framework for mastery is grounded in the actions of deliberate practice.

Afterword

I hope you have enjoyed reading *Deliberate Practice for Creative Writers*. If so, I'd appreciate it if you could post a review or rating online. Short reviews really make a difference and help me, as an independent author and teacher, to publish more books like these, which help to bridge the gap between general writing workshops and the next level of writing craft.

I'd love to hear about how you use deliberate practice, and your discoveries and examples.

Get in touch with me by email: **info@method-writing.com**

You're also welcome to join my Method Writing mailing list, for occasional newsletters, advance review copies, writing tips, and research findings: **www.method-writing.com**.

Many thanks and happy writing!

Jules

Glossary

Active/passive voice

In grammar, in *active voice*, the person or thing doing the action comes first (e.g. "She wrote the story"). In *passive voice*, the entity receiving the action comes first (e.g. "The story was written").

Characterization

The creation and development of a story character's personality, traits, and motivations.

Cloze

An exercise technique where words are removed from a text, and the writer fills in the gaps.

Context

The background, surrounding details, or bigger picture.

Eustress/distress

Eustress: a small level of positive stress that can help to build resilience. Distress: negative stress.

Flow

In writing or music, a smooth movement that keeps the reader or listener engaged, and creates a natural, enjoyable pace.

Form

In writing, the structural and shape features of a piece (e.g. a sonnet typically has 14 lines; a monologue is a first-person form).

Freewriting

Unfiltered, continuous writing to generate ideas without editing or judgment.

Genre

Means *kind, type.* Use to refer to categories and styles of literature (e.g. fiction, horror, romance).

Grammar

The rules governing sentence structure and word usage in language.

Head-hopping

Shifting the story viewpoint between characters within a single scene, often confusing for readers.

Idiolect

An individual's unique way of using language.
Immersive
In writing, engaging your reader deeply by creating a vivid, absorbing world.

Iteration

A quick, repeated process of refining ideas or drafts to improve clarity and impact.

Metaphor

A figure of speech that directly compares two dissimilar things, saying one *is* the other to add meaning (e.g. "Time is a thief"). Unlike a *simile*, it does not use "like" or "as."

Modal

In grammar, words that express possibility, permission, obligation, or necessity (e.g. *can, must, might, should*).

Multimodal

Using multiple modes of communication (e.g. written, audio, visuals, textiles) to create meaning.

Osmosis

In learning, absorbing knowledge or style through exposure, rather than direct study.

Parts of speech

Categories of words, such as nouns, verbs, and adjectives; each plays a role in sentence construction (see **Part 5** for more detail).

Plant/payoff

Planting a hint or clue early in the story, and resolving it later for impact (see also **Withholding**).

Practice

The act of regularly engaging in a skill to improve. It can also refer to the specific approach, methods, or philosophy behind an activity, as in a meditation practice or arts practice.

Puppeting

A writing issue where characters feel unnatural or "wooden" because the writer's control over their actions and dialogue is too obvious, in an otherwise naturalistic style.

Rhythm

The beat or flow of language, influenced by sentence length, punctuation, and word choice.

Salience

Making elements stand out in text, drawing the reader's attention.

Scene

A sequence within a story where characters interact in a single setting or moment.

Signposts

Cues or markers that help to guide readers through a text or story structure, particularly spatial or temporal.

Spatial

Relates to the physical arrangement or location within a setting.

Stress

In writing technique, the emphasis placed on words or ideas within a sentence for impact.

Subtext

The underlying unspoken meaning or implication which isn't stated directly, but inferred by the reader.

Syntax

A subset of grammar, referring to the arrangement of words and phrases to create coherent sentences.

Temporal

Relating to time, especially in structuring the progression of a story.

Tropes

Commonly used themes or conventions in storytelling (e.g. hero's journey).

Transmit/receive

In writing, the exchange of meaning between writer and reader.

Visualization

The act of making something visible, whether by using imagination to create mental images, invoking the reader's imagination, or applying visual techniques for learning and memorization.

Viewpoint

The character perspective from which the story is narrated (e.g. first person, third person), mindset or mental landscape.

Withholding

Deliberately delaying information to create suspense or curiosity (see also **Plant/payoff**.

Endnotes

1   Klee, P. (1968) *Pedagogical Sketchbook*. Translated by S. Moholy-Nagy. New York: Praeger.
2   Fogg, B.J. (2020) *Tiny Habits: The Small Changes That Change Everything*. Boston: Houghton Mifflin Harcourt.
3   Kellogg, R.T. & Whiteford, A.P. (2009) Training advanced writing skills: The case for deliberate practice. *Educational Psychologist*, 44(4), pp.250-266. This research study highlights how deliberate practice can improve writing skills by focusing on specific weaknesses and practising them intensively. MacArthur, C.A., Graham, S. & Fitzgerald, J. (eds.) (2006) *Handbook of writing research*. New York: Guilford Press. This handbook compiles research studies on writing instruction, with specific reference to how deliberate practice principles can be applied to writing teaching at different education levels.
4   King, S. (2006) *Cell*. London: Hodder & Stoughton.
5   King, S. (2006) *Cell*. London: Hodder & Stoughton.
6   le Carré, J. (1974) *Tinker Tailor Soldier Spy*. London: Hodder & Stoughton.
7   "In the middle of things" or "into the midst of things" is a translation of the Latin phrase *in medias res*. It comes from the Roman poet Horace's work *Ars Poetica* (The Art of Poetry), one of the earliest discussions of writing craft.
8   le Carré, J. (1974) *Tinker Tailor Soldier Spy*. London: Hodder & Stoughton.
9   Introduced by Julia Cameron in Cameron, J. (1992) *The Artist's Way*. New York: Tarcher/Putnam.
10   Horne, J. (2020) *Nanonovels*. Kelso: Texthouse. See also the *Nanonovels* notebook for your own microfiction experiments.

11   de Bernières, L. (1994) *Captain Corelli's Mandolin*. London: Secker & Warburg.

12   Lofthouse, T. (2019) Louis de Bernières. https://www.timeandleisure.co.uk/louis-de-bernieres/ [Accessed 30 October 2024].

13   Fogg, B.J. (2020) *Tiny Habits: The Small Changes That Change Everything*. Boston: Houghton Mifflin Harcourt.

14   James, H. (1978) *The Tragic Muse*. Penguin Modern Classics. London: Penguin Books.

15   von Trier, L. and Leth, J. (2003) *The Five Obstructions* [film]. Denmark: Zentropa Real.

16   Quoted in Bey, K, Interview with Simon Stephens. *Voicemag*. https://www.voicemag.uk/interview/1191/interview-with-simon-stephens-playwright [Accessed 27 June 2024]

17   Skinner, B.F. (1974) *About Behaviorism*. New York: Alfred A. Knopf.

18   Harris, J.R. (1998) *The Nurture Assumption: Why Children Turn Out the Way They Do*. New York: Free Press.

19   Pinker, S. (2002) *The Blank Slate: The Modern Denial of Human Nature*. New York: Viking.

20   Ericsson, K.A., Krampe, R.T. & Tesch-Römer, C. (1993) The role of deliberate practice in the acquisition of expert performance. *Psychological Review*, 100(3), pp.363-406.

21   Gladwell, M. (2008) *Outliers: The Story of Success*. New York: Little, Brown and Company.

22   Taylor, D. (2022) Ray Bradbury's greatest writing advice. Literary Hub. Available at: https://lithub.com/ray-bradburys-greatest-writing-advice/ [Accessed 21 Sep. 2024].

23   The Story, 2024. Daily routines of famous writers. The Story. Available at: https://thestory.au/articles/daily-routines-famous-writers/ [Accessed 21 Sep. 2024].

24   Goins, J., 2017. *Real artists don't starve: Timeless strategies for thriving in the new creative age*. Nashville, TN: Thomas Nelson.

25   National Novel Writing Month (NaNoWriMo) (2023) National Novel Writing Month. Available at: https://nanowrimo.org [Accessed 29 October 2024].

26   Pressfield, S. (2012) *The War of Art: Break Through the Blocks and Win Your Inner Creative Battles*. New York: Black Irish Entertainment LLC.

27 Some people can't rely on memory formation because their brains can't form new declarative memories. This is a debilitating condition, *anterograde amnesia*, where even close friends and family are strangers on each new encounter.

28 Moffat, S. (Writer) & Ford, D. (Director) (2014) Listen (Season 8, Episode 4). *Doctor Who*. [TV Series]. BBC.
29 Moffat, S. (Writer) & Ford, D. (Director) (2014) Listen (Season 8, Episode 4). *Doctor Who*. [TV Series]. BBC.
30 Goggins, D. (2018) *Can't Hurt Me: Master Your Mind and Defy the Odds*. Austin, TX: Lioncrest Publishing.
31 Murakami, H. (2009) *What I Talk About When I Talk About Running*. London: Vintage.

32 J.K. Rowling. The pseudonymous Galbraith's first novel, *Cormoran Strike*, was released anonymously, and his true identity revealed after its release.

33 This field, called *forensic linguistics*, uses a data analysis process called *stylometry* to attribute authorship to a text.

34 Gladwell, M. (2008) *Outliers: The Story of Success*. 1st ed. New York: Little, Brown and Company.
35 Ericsson, K.A., Krampe, R.T. and Tesch-Römer, C. (1993) The role of deliberate practice in the acquisition of expert performance. *Psychological Review*, 100(3). For a more accessible overview, see Ericsson, K.A. and Pool, R. (2016) *Peak: Secrets from the New Science of Expertise*. London: Bodley Head.
36 Tharp, T. (2009) *The Creative Habit: Learn It and Use It For Life*. New York: Simon & Schuster.
37 Lally, P., van Jaarsveld, C.H.M., Potts, H.W.W. and Wardle, J. (2010) How are habits formed: Modelling habit formation in the real world. *European Journal of Social Psychology*, 40(6).
38 Fogg, B.J. (2020) *Tiny Habits: The Small Changes That Change Everything*. Boston: Houghton Mifflin Harcourt.
39 Kafka, F. (1925) *The Trial*. Translated from German by M. Mitchell, 2009. London: Vintage Classics.
40 Vonnegut, K. (2004) Kurt Vonnegut Lecture, Case Western Reserve University [video]. Available at: https://youtu.be/4_RUgnC1lm8 [Accessed 24 September 2024].
41 Jockers, M. and Archer, J. (2017) *The Bestseller Code: Anatomy of the Blockbuster Novel*. London: Penguin Books.

42   Lamott, A. (2020) *Bird by Bird: Some Instructions on Writing and Life*. Edinburgh: Canongate.

43   Goldberg, N. (2010) *Writing Down the Bones: Freeing the Writer Within*. Boston: Shambhala Publications.

44   Woolf, V. (1928) *Orlando: A Biography*. London: Hogarth Press.

45   Bradbury, R. (1990) *Zen in the Art of Writing*. Santa Barbara: Joshua Odell Editions.

46   Cameron, J. (1992) *The Artist's Way: A Spiritual Path to Higher Creativity*. New York: Jeremy P. Tarcher/Putnam.

47   Hammond, W. and Steward, D., eds. (2008) *Verbatim Verbatim: Techniques in Contemporary Documentary Theatre*. London: Oberon Books.

48   See The Open University/BFI course, *Reading the Screen*. https://www.open.ac.uk/courses/short-courses/axs003#details. [Accessed 30 October 2024]

49   "Cloze" comes from the concept of "closure" in Gestalt psychology. It describes the process of completing language examples with missing words. The term was coined in 1953 by Wilson L. Taylor, an American psychologist and education researcher.

50   le Carré, J. (1974) *Tinker Tailor Soldier Spy*. London: Hodder & Stoughton.

51   Atwood, M. (2013) *Oryx and Crake*. London: Virago.

52   Mantel, H. (2009) *Wolf Hall*. London: Fourth Estate.

53   *Text* in an academic context can refer not just to written words, but to anything that can be "read" or interpreted, including films, paintings, performances, and cultural practices.

54   Atwood, M. (1981) 'Spelling' in *True Stories: Poems*. Toronto: Oxford University Press.

55   A more granular approach could start with letters. I see them less as units, more as particles.

56   Klee, P. (1968). *Pedagogical Sketchbook*. Translated by S. Moholy-Nagy. New York: Praeger.

57   The MRC Cognition and Brain Sciences Unit at Cambridge, involving researchers like Dr. Norris, explores the relationship between working memory and chunking.

58   Hammond, W. and Steward, D., eds. (2008) *Verbatim Verbatim: Contemporary Documentary Theatre*. London: Oberon Books.

59   *The Terminator* (1984) [Film]. Directed by James Cameron.

60 Carroll, L. (1865/2022) *Alice's Adventures in Wonderland*. London: Penguin Classics.

61 *The Shining* (1980) [Film]. Directed by Stanley Kubrick.

62 *Jerry Maguire* (1996) [Film]. Directed by Cameron Crowe.

63 *The Simpsons* (1989-), *Buffy the Vampire Slayer* (1997-2003).

64 *Little Britain* (2003-2006).

65 *The Fast Show* (1994-1997).

66 Joey Tribbiani in *Friends* (1994-2004).

67 *RuPaul's Drag Race* (2009-) [TV Series]. Created by RuPaul.

68 *Casablanca* (1942) [Film]. Directed by Michael Curtiz.

69 *The King's Speech* (2010) [Film]. Directed by Tom Hooper.

70 *Lost in Translation* (2003) [Film]. Directed by Sofia Coppola.

71 *The Silence of the Lambs* (1991) [Film]. Directed by Jonathan Demme.

72 *Forrest Gump* (1994) [Film]. Directed by Robert Zemeckis.

73 *Good Will Hunting* (1997) [Film]. Directed by Gus Van Sant.

74 Designed by Tim-Berners-Lee, who invented the World Wide Web in 1991. The idea was introduced in his seminal article, *The Semantic Web*, published in *Scientific American* in 2001. It provides a model for representing information, using entities and relationships between them. His Resource Description Framework (RDF) uses the categories subject, predicate, object – linguistic terms from traditional grammar.

75 Adjectives and adverbs are both types of *modifiers*. This is a general term to describe a word or phrase that adds clarity or detail to another word or phrase.

76 Note that the same word can have different functions in different contexts. So, outside in the phrase "go outside" is an adverb, as it modifies the verb, *to go*. But outside in the phrase "outside the house" is a preposition, as it's linked to the noun, *house*.

77 Articles belong to a class of words called *determiners*. Other determiners include t*his/these/those; my/your/her/their; some/any/much/few/ several; which/what/whose*. Like articles, they add specificity to the noun (often quantity, or ownership of things). Numbers can be determiners: *three owls, the first girl on the moon*.

78 For example, "Stop!" could be seen as an interjection, or a command (an imperative, in grammar terms). Or as both! Linguists sometimes refer to such words as *multifunctional* or *polyfunctional*.

79   This effect is often used in comedy.

80   Forster, E.M. (1984) *Aspects of the Novel*. Harmondsworth: Pelican.

81   Miller, G.A. (1956) The magical number seven, plus or minus two: Some limits on our capacity for processing information. *Psychological Review*, 63(2).

82   Cowan, N. (2001) The magical number 4 in short-term memory: A reconsideration of mental storage capacity. *Behavioral and Brain Sciences*, 24(1).

83   Fowler, H.W. (2015) *A Dictionary of Modern English Usage*. Edited by D. Crystal. Oxford: Oxford University Press.

84   du Maurier, D. (2003) *Rebecca*. London: Virago Press.

85   Poe, E.A. (2012) *The Raven*. London: Penguin Classics.

86   Von Restorff, H. (1933) Über die Wirkung von Bereichsbildungen im Spurenfeld. *Psychologische Forschung*, 18(1). Available at: https://en.wikipedia.org/wiki/Von_Restorff_effect [Accessed: 28 October 2024].

87   Paivio, A. (1971) *Imagery and Verbal Processes*. New York: Holt, Rinehart & Winston.

88   Gardner, J. (1983) *The Art of Fiction: Notes on Craft for Young Writers*. New York: Vintage Books.

89   Horne, J. (2018) *Dramatic Techniques for Creative Writers*. Kelso: Texthouse.

90   Dr. Seuss (1960) *Green Eggs and Ham*. New York: Random House.

91   Kleon, A. (2010) *Newspaper Blackout*. New York: Harper Perennial.

92   Calvino, I. (1979) *If on a winter's night a traveler*. Translated from Italian by W. Weaver (1981) London: Harcourt Brace Jovanovich.

93   Perec, G. (1978) *Life: A User's Manual*. Translated from French by D. Bellos (1987) London: Harvill Press.

94   A famous novel-length lipogram is Georges Perec's *La Disparition*, which is written entirely without the letter "e". Perec, G. (1969) *La Disparition*. Paris: Denoël. The main English translation, by Gilbert Adair, is called *A Void*. Perec, G. (1994) *A Void*. Translated from French by G. Adair. London: Harvill Press.

95   For a notable example of a novel written predominantly in a single, unbroken sentence, see Ellmann, L. (2019) *Ducks, Newburyport*. Norwich: Galley Beggar Press.

96   Sometimes, there are commas around the *which* clause, This depends on whether it's a defining or non-defining relative clause.

97   Gray, S. (2004) *The Smoking Diaries*. London: Granta Books.

98   OpenAI (2024) ChatGPT. Available at: https://chat.openai.com/ [Accessed 25 September 2024].

99   Beats and uniting are based on the teachings of the Russian theatre director, Konstantin Stanislavski, and are discussed further in my book, *Dramatic Techniques for Creative Writers.* Stanislavski's original teachings can be found in Stanislavski, C. (2013) *An Actor Prepares.* London: Bloomsbury Academic.

100   *The Proposal* (2009) directed by Anne Fletcher. USA: Touchstone Pictures.

101   Ericsson, A. and Pool, R. (2016) *Peak: Secrets from the New Science of Expertise. London: Vintage.*

102   Horne, J. (2020) *Nanonovels.* Kelso: Texthouse.

103   Fogg, B.J. (2020) *Tiny Habits: The Small Changes That Change Everything.* Boston: Houghton Mifflin Harcourt.

104   Gladwell, M. (2008) *Outliers: The Story of Success.* New York: Little, Brown and Company.

105   Dweck, C. (2006) *Mindset: The New Psychology of Success.* New York: Random House.

106   Greene, R. (2012) Mastery. London: Profile Books.

107   Syme, B. (2018) *Dear Writer, You Need to Quit. Better-Faster Academy.*

108   Pressfield, S. (2012) *Turning Pro: Tap Your Inner Power and Create Your Life's Work.* New York: Black Irish Entertainment.

More Books by Jules Horne

Dramatic Techniques for Creative Writers

"Accessible, clearly written, and really, really helpful for fiction writers of all levels of experience. I've read a lot of books for writers in the past few years. This is one of the best."

Josie Johnston

This practical guide to dramatic concepts will give you confidence in structure, plotting and character, and may even blow your mind. At the very least, you'll kick yourself for not discovering them sooner.

Also available as an audiobook.
Find out more on my Method Writing website:

method-writing.com/books

Writing for Audiobooks

"Audiobooks are the fastest-growing segment in publishing, but writing for audio first is a skill that few writers have needed to learn. Until now. If you want to make sure your writing resonates for this growing audience, Jules's book will give you useful tips for adjusting your words and reaching listeners. Highly recommended!"

Joanna Penn, The Creative Penn

How to prepare your writing for audio and podcast production, using professional radio writing techniques and tips to make your words sparkle. Learn how to write from an audio-first perspective, use flow words and phrases, handle visual book elements, hook listeners and keep them engaged – and lots more from the world of radio and podcast writing.

Also available as an audiobook.
Find out more on my Method Writing website:

method-writing.com/books

How to Launch a Freelance Copywriting Business

"A godsend for me... a clear, comprehensive, friendly and approachable down-to-earth manual... this book has it all. Highly recommended."

Malcolm Pryce, novelist

Practical handbook with the nuts and bolts of starting a copywriting business, plus a companion workbook to jumpstart your process and keep you on track.

Also available as an audiobook.
Find out more on my Method Writing website:

www.method-writing.com/books

Nanonovels

A genre-busting experiment in storytelling and the mystery of creativity, inspired by a magpie collection of vintage print books, in the year that Kindle changed books for ever. *150 days. 150 stories.* Each one a tiny flash fiction gem. Ready to try the Nanonovel experiment with your own writing? Read *Nanonovels*, get yourself a *Challenge Workbook*, and go and write your own.

Nanonovels 30-Day Challenge Workbook

Need help to get started with your writing? This *Nanonovel Challenge Workbook* will help you to dive in and write your own microfiction with just five minutes of deliberate practice a day.

Join the Method Writing mailing list:

www.method-writing.com/books

Printed in Great Britain
by Amazon

57921523R00129